Nymph Fishing

Dave Hughes

photographed by Jim Schollmeyer

illustrated by Richard Bunse

flies tied by John Rodriguez

Frank Amato

PORTLAND

Dedication

To Ted Leeson, admirable author, and an excellent friend with whom to explore the world of water and the world of words.

Acknowledgements

Rick Hafele, with whom I co-authored *The Complete Book of Western Hatches*, urged me into fishing with nymphs, usually by stepping into the same water I had already fished fruitlessly some other way and abruptly catching a bunch of trout. He also taught me all I know about the aquatic insects trout eat, and that I now imitate most often when I fish nymphs. I would also like to thank Keith Burkhart, owner of the Valley Fly Fisher in Salem, Oregon, for support on this and other projects. And thank you again, John, for rescuing me by tying the beautiful flies in this book.

Dave Hughes is the author of *Dry Fly Fishing* (Frank Amato Publications, Inc., 1994) in this same series of books. His many other books include *American Fly Tying Manual*, *An Angler's Astoria*, and the four-book *Strategies for Streams* series. He writes the "Fly Fishing Success" column for *Fly Rod & Reel*, and contributes regularly to *Flyfishing* magazine. He is a life member of Oregon Trout, the Federation of Flyfishers, the Flyfishers Club of Oregon, the Santiam Fly Casters, the Anglers Club of Portland, and his home club, the Rainland Fly Casters in Astoria, Oregon.

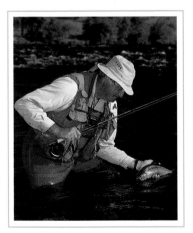

Jim Schollmeyer is co-author of *Fly Casting Illustrated in Color* with Frank Amato, and author of *Hatch Guide for the Lower Deschutes*. His photos appear regularly in *Field & Stream*, *Flyfishing*, and *Fly Fisherman* magazines. He photographed *Dry Fly Fishing*, and took the acclaimed plates in Randle Scott Stetzer's *Flies: The Best One Thousand*. Jim's photography is also featured in *Saltwater Flies: Over 700 of the Best* by Deke Meyer and *Fish Flies* by Terry Hellekson. Schollmeyer is a guide on Oregon's Deschutes River. He is a popular speaker and slide show presenter at fishing club meetings, banquets, and sportsmens shows. He makes his home in Salem, Oregon.

Published in 1995 by Frank Amato Publications, Inc.
P.O. Box 82112, Portland, Oregon 97282
(503) 653-8108

Softbound ISBN: 1-57188-002-X

Book Design: Tony Amato

Printed in Hong Kong

5 7 9 10 8 6 4

Table of Contents

Chapter 1

❧

Success with Nymphs

Nymphing is said to be difficult. It's harder to take trout on nymphs down below than it is to take them on dry flies up top, or so that rumor goes.

The rumor can be true. It can also be false.

More years ago than I care to count, back before strike indicators came into common use, everything written about nymphing revealed the terrible difficulties involved. I fished them rarely in those days, and timidly when I did, because of all the fearful stuff I read. My fear and timidity were both set aside in a single day on the Big Hole River, in Montana. That was the day my friend Ernest "Tex" Baxter stepped up to an immense, choppy riffle and announced that he was going to fish it with a nymph.

Tex Baxter plays a nymph-hooked trout in a Big Hole River riffle.

Learning to fish nymphs will increase the number of trout you get to hold in your hands.

squirted into the air on Tex's first cast. He had a dozen more rainbows up and dancing as he waded and fished his swinging nymph down the length of that Big Hole River riffle. I watched awhile, applauded a lot. Then I forgot all my own timidities, stepped into the riffle behind Tex, and fished a nymph the same way he did. I quickly prodded some trout of my own into the air, and discovered that nymphing did not need to be difficult in order to fool a few fish.

Nothing could be easier than the way Tex fished his nymph that day on the Big Hole. To this day I use nymphs fished on the downstream swing to fool lots of smart trout, on waters all across this continent, and on a few others.

Nymphing wisdom at the time called for wading in at the bottom end of a riffle, and fishing upstream with a floating line, the same as it would be done with a dry fly, but without the advantage of being able to see the visible take. I watched and wondered how Tex was going to pull this off. I knew he would never be able to spot a take to his nymph in such rough water.

His line tip might dart that imperceptible inch everybody wrote about, back then, but he'd never see it. He might get hits, but he'd never know it.

Tex confounded me and all those early writers by stepping in at the top end of the riffle, not the bottom. He cast straight out across it, not upstream. I watched while he let his nymph simply swing down and around on a line that was not tight, but cinched up enough to relay news of a take in the form of a thump on the rod. Of course, I knew this wouldn't work. I'd read how foolish it was to expect a trout to take a nymph swinging across the current rather than drifting freely with it.

The trout hadn't read it. One went whap! and

Trout are said to spend 90 percent of their time feeding on natural nymphs and larvae right along the bottom. I doubt that the number is truly that dramatic. More likely, they spend around 75 percent to 80 percent of their time feeding on the bottom. When they do, however, they can be tricked with

Trout spend most of their time holding and feeding along the bottom, where they're most susceptible to being taken with nymphs.

nymphs, and most often only with nymphs. It's easy to see that you'd be wasting more than half of your trout fishing opportunities if you failed to fish nymphs.

Learning to fish nymphs will greatly increase your ability to adapt to various fishing conditions, and therefore increase your chances of catching trout in a wide range of situations. As a result, it will reduce the number of days when you trot home fishless. That's not a bad reason to learn nymphing, but I like to look at nymph fishing in a slightly different way. By learning to fish nymphs with more consistent success, you automatically increase the number of days on which you assess the wind and weather of your chances, and conclude that with nymphs you have some hope of catching a few fish. You therefore decide to hoist your rod and get out fishing much more often.

Nymphing, looked at in this way, will greatly increase the number of days that you deliver yourself out to a stream during the season. It's slightly peripheral that you also increase the number of trout that you catch when you get there. Being prompted to go fishing more often is in itself a measure of increased success. Nymph fishing will do that for you.

Nymphing can remain as simple an endeavor as Tex kept it on the Big Hole River. You'll still catch trout. It can also become as complicated as you want it. With the advent of strike indicator and split shot nymphing, your trout fishing can become truly technical, and also almost constantly effective.

Nymph fishing skills, and consequent nymph fishing success, are on a continuum, from simple at one end to complex at the other. As soon as you begin fishing nymphs, you'll insert yourself somewhere on this continuum and begin advancing along it, solving new situations, catching more fish as you amble along. No matter where you find yourself along the line at the start, you'll catch some trout on nymphs. As you advance, you'll always have some fresh new fishing success behind you, giving you a sense of satisfaction, and some new fishing situation needing to be solved ahead of you, promising a challenge.

In nymph fishing for trout, there are always new things to learn. In the end, it's always the streams and the stillwaters and the trout themselves that prompt us into discovering something new about nymphing, and therefore about catching more and larger trout.

Trout taken on nymphs fished along the bottom are often larger than those caught on dry flies fished at the surface.

Chapter 2

❧

Tackle for Nymphing

The best outfit for nymphing is probably one that you already own. Your current fly rod was likely chosen to fish well on the waters you fish most often. If it's big water, most likely you've got a rod 9 feet long that casts a 6- or 7-weight line. If it's medium water, chances are you already own an 8-1/2 to 9 footer balanced to a 5- or 6-weight line. If you fish small water most often, it's likely you own a light outfit: a 7-1/2 to 8-1/2 foot rod that propels a 4- or 5-weight line.

If you intend to continue fishing the same kinds of water when you take up nymphing, or when you seek to improve the

nymphing you're already doing, then you probably own the nymph outfit that will be perfect for the water you'll be fishing most often. If that's true, stick with what you've got, and go fishing.

Rod Selection

If you feel the need to buy a new rod and reel specifically for nymphing, the best all-around outfit might be lighter than you'd expect. In nymphing, it's usually a mistake to cast long,

The best nymphing rod is likely to be the one that you already own.

more than about 40 feet. A long cast increases the chances of tangles, reduces your control of the drift, and also reduces the chance you'll detect a take when you get one. A light to medium rod will almost always cast as far as you want, when you're fishing nymphs.

The all-around outfit: The best rod for the general run of nymph fishing would be graphite, 8-1/2 to 9 feet long, balanced to cast a double-taper 5-weight or weight-forward 6-weight line. That's about the same rod you'd use to fish the general run of dry flies, wet flies, and small streamers on average sized trout streams. It will be a very versatile

An excellent rod for average nymphing, one that will serve for other types of fishing as well, would be 8-1/2 to 9 feet long, balanced to a 5- or 6-weight line.

outfit. You'll be able to accomplish almost all of your trout fishing with it. Most experienced fly fishermen—guides and writers—own a rod 8-1/2 to 9 feet long that casts a double-taper 5-weight line or weight-forward 6-weight. Catch them astream, by surprise, and that's what they'll be using.

If you fish most often on streams smaller than average, you might do better by purchasing an 8 foot rod balanced to a double-taper 4-weight line. If you fish large water most often, you'll be better off buying a 9 to 9-1/2 foot rod balanced to a weight-forward 7-weight line.

For fishing large rivers, at times with heavy nymphs or lots of weight on the leader, you'll be served better with a stout rod: 9 to 9-1/2 feet long for a 7- or 8-weight line.

The heavy nymphing rod: If you fish a lot with large, heavily weighted nymphs, you'll be well served by a second rod. This kind of fishing is done most often on big Western rivers, with size 4 and 6 nymphs that have 20 to 30 wraps of lead wire wrapped around their shanks. These are often used to bang the banks while drifting in a boat. The demand is for a line heavy enough to command the fly, and a rod slow enough to cast that line with a patient, open loop. If you cast heavy flies with a fast rod, you lose control and wind up whapping yourself in the head with them.

The perfect rod for what I call *lifting weights* should be 9 to 9-1/2 feet long, balanced to a weight-forward 7- or 8-weight line. One way to acquire a slow rod, if you already own a rod that is fairly fast, is to overline it. Arm a fast 6-weight rod with a double-taper 7-weight or a weight-forward 8-weight, and you instantly slow it down.

Mistakes to avoid: Don't buy a rod that is too short. Line control on the water is critical to nymphing. 8-1/2 to 9 foot rods let you mend and tend your drifts better than 7 to 7-1/2 foot rods. A rod shorter than 8 feet is a slight handicap in nearly all forms of nymphing.

If you own a fast rod and want a slow one, simply overline it one or two line weights, which will also help you carry heavy nymphs in the air.

Don't buy a rod with an action so fast it feels stiff when you cast it. The average rod on the market today is designed for distance casting with tight loops, and is too fast for nymphing. If you cast nymphs with a tight loop, you're going to end up with tangles when you add split shot and strike indicators to your leader. Buy a rod with a medium to medium-fast action, not one so fast it feels stiff. The slightly slower rod allows you to open up your casting loops, so all those trinkets on your leader don't get tangled in the air.

Lines

Nearly all of your nymphing—more than 90 percent—can be best done with a floating line. Weight, whether tied into the fly or added later to the leader, is used to sink the fly quickly. The floating line, as opposed to one that sinks, gives you a visual fix on the position of the fly, and far more control over its drift.

Your first line should be a double-taper or weight-forward floater. It should balance the rod on a short cast: 20 to 40 feet. Don't buy the line that balances your rod on a 60 to 70 foot cast. You won't enjoy much success fishing at those ranges with nymphs.

Choose a weight-forward floating line if you'll be fishing the outfit primarily with nymphs. The weight-forward taper has most of

A fast rod is a mistake for nymph fishing. You need a rod that lets you loft a slow backcast with an open loop, to avoid tangling weighted nymphs, split shot, and indicators.

its casting weight in the first 30 feet of line. This weight will help you handle heavy nymphs, split shot, and strike indicators with more authority, at short range, than a double-taper line, which has the same amount of weight spread over the first 40 to 45 feet. If you'll use the same line to fish the full range of dry flies, wets, nymphs, and streamers, then consider a double-taper line for the added control it gives you once the cast has landed on the water.

For your heavy outfit, the one used for lifting weighted nymphs and lobbing them toward the banks from a boat, use a weight-forward line, and be sure that it's heavy enough to slow the rod into a moderate action, rather than fast. For my own fishing, I use a double-taper line on my light outfit and a weight-forward line on my heavy outfit.

The only other line you'll want for nymphing on moving water is a weight-forward 10 foot sinking-tip line for your heavy outfit. You'll use this in just a couple of kinds of nymph fishing on big rivers, and a lot for nymphing on lakes.

Your line is the critical component of your fly fishing outfit. Buy the best you can afford. The difference in price between an excellent line and a cheap one is less than twenty dollars. The performance of a poor line can cost you a lot more than that out on the stream or lake.

Your reel should be a single-action, large enough to hold the chosen line plus 100 yards of backing. An extra spool with a sink-tip line will complete your outfit for most nymphing.

Reels

Your reel should be a single action, large enough to hold the chosen fly line plus at least 100 yards of backing line. If you choose to purchase the extra sinking-tip line for your heavy rod, then you'll need an extra spool for your reel to hold that line plus backing.

The reel should have a smooth and dependable drag. This is largely the variable that improves when you spend more money to buy a better reel. The rule on reels is to get the right size to hold your line and backing, then buy the best quality you can afford in order to increase its dependability and the smoothness of its drag.

Leaders

If you're fishing a nymph without indicator and split shot, then you should use the same tapered leader and tippet you'd use for a dry fly or wet fly in the same situation. Refer to the chart on this page to choose the correct diameter tippet to balance the fly size you're using.

Leaders for indicator and split shot nymphing are so varied, and so dependent on the water you'll be fishing, that they're covered in Chapter 4, "Rigging to Fish Nymphs".

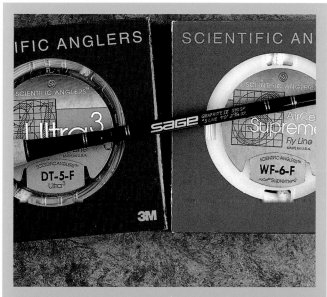

Rods are rated for the double-taper line they'll cast best. If you choose a weight-forward line, it's nearly always necessary to go up one line weight to balance the rod properly. A rod that casts well with a DT5F line will usually require a WF6F to load right. No matter what your rod rating says, cast a new rod with lines one size heavier and one size lighter than the rating before you choose a line for it. Because of the short casts used in nymphing, and most other trout fishing, it's common that the best line is one weight heavier than the one called for by the rod manufacturer, even in double-taper.

Tippet Diameter and Fly Size

Diameter	X number	Fly Size
(in 1/1,000")		
.011"	0X	1/0, 1, 2
.010"	1X	4, 6, 8
.009"	2X	6, 8, 10
.008"	3X	10, 12, 14
.007"	4X	12, 14, 16
.006"	5X	14, 16, 18, 20
.005"	6X	18, 20, 22, 24
.004"	7X	20, 22, 24, 26

*I*f you fish nymphs because trout spend 75 percent to 80 percent of their time feeding on natural nymphs along the bottom, then it makes sense to base your fly selection on what's down there, being eaten by trout. If they're feeding on lots of different things, and your fly looks at least roughly like something they've just eaten, then it's likely trout will take it. If they're feeding selectively on just one food form, then they're not likely to accept your fly unless it looks a lot like that particular insect or crustacean.

Non-Selective Feeding

Trout are rarely selective when they feed on or near the bottom. On the surface, trout often see a single stage of a single species of insect, say a mayfly dun. Your dry fly must match it to fool fish. When trout hold and feed at depth, however, they usually see a wide variety of natural nymphs, larvae, and crustaceans tumbling along. They intercept whatever comes their way if it looks alive.

Trout feeding on the bottom in a fast riffle or run are rarely selective, and will nearly always take a generic nymph if it is fished right.

Trout feeding non-selectively are most likely to accept your fly if it looks like it belongs among the many naturals they've been taking lately. They're most likely to reject it if it has no resemblance to anything they've seen in days.

With this theory of general selectivity in mind, you can select and carry a narrow range of nymph dressings that average the size, shape, and color spectrum of natural nymphs, larvae, and crustaceans. Fish one or another of these generic dressings anywhere in the world, and you'll be able to fool at least a few trout. Most often, you'll be able to catch more fish on a generic pattern than you can on a precise imitation of something that does not happen to be abundant along the bottom at the moment.

If a particular insect is more abundant than others on bottom stones, it's wise to choose a generic dressing that looks a little like it in size, form, and color.

Generic nymphs: The four most common colors among natural nymphs, larvae, and crustaceans found in streams are gray, green, tan, and brown. Four of the most successful nymph patterns of all time cover these colors. The Muskrat has a gray muskrat fur body. The Herl Nymph has a body of green peacock herl. Dave Whitlock's famous Fox Squirrel has a body of blended tan fur and bright Antron synthetic. The Gold Ribbed Hare's Ear has a body of brown fur. All four patterns capture the shape of many natural trout foods.

You won't go wrong building your first collection of nymphs around these four dressings. Tie or buy each pattern in sizes 10 through 16, all of them slightly weighted.

Four nymphs that cover the basic colors of naturals, and that have a well-earned reputation for catching lots of trout, include the Muskrat, Herl Nymph, Fox Squirrel, and Gold Ribbed Hare's Ear.

The average size nymph: It's a common mistake to think that because you fish nymphs down deep, you'd better use fairly large flies or they'll never get noticed by trout. It's far from true. Trout make a living seeing and eating whatever the bottom currents deliver to them.

The average insect delivered is a lot smaller than you think. Sure, a few stonefly nymphs and cased caddis larvae are so large you'd imitate them with size 6 and 8 flies,

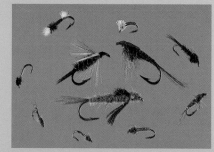

but most mayfly nymphs, free-living caddis larvae, midge larvae, and myriad other food forms are less than half that size. Add all the early life stages of the larger groups, and what you get are trout feeding on average bites best imitated on size 14 or 16 hooks.

Gaze into the fly boxes of an expert nymph fisherman sometime, and you'll see row after row of size 14 and 16 nymphs interspersed with a few scattered dressings that are tied on size 8, 10, and 12 hooks: the size nymphs most of us use most of the time.

If you learn nothing more from this chapter, learn to reduce the size of the nymphs that you fish most often down to the average size bites that trout eat most often. You'll instantly begin catching a lot more trout.

Imitative Nymphs
for Selective Feeding

If a single insect or other food form dominates the waters you're fishing, you'll do best if you imitate it with your nymph. This is not common. When it happens, however, you'll catch trout only if you're prepared for it.

Giant salmonfly nymphs migrate across the bottom of big rivers, headed for emergence on shore. Trout key on them when they do. Green caddis larvae can tumble so abundantly along the bottom in fast water that trout become selective to them. During damselfly nymph migrations in lakes, trout accept little that doesn't look like them.

These are just examples of events that cause trout to become selective to certain nymphs. Your fly boxes, built around a few generic dressings that average out the size and color spectrum of naturals, should also contain a few patterns that match specific underwater food forms that you find on your waters. Samples include Kaufmann's Black Stone for the giant salmonfly nymph, the Green Caddis Larva for the caddis, and the Pheasant Tail for times when *Baetis* mayflies hatch, but trout refuse dry flies.

Giant salmonfly nymph . . .

. . . and its imitation, Kaufmann's Black Stone.

A caddis larva, the green rock worm . . .

. . . and its imitation, the Green Caddis Larva.

A little olive mayfly nymph . . .

. . . and its imitation, the Pheasant Tail Nymph.

Collecting naturals: You'll increase your knowledge of trout streams, and improve your fishing, if you collect at least briefly in the waters you intend to fish. This gives you a look at the actu-al foods that trout might be eating. Do this before you begin fishing, or whenever you're nymphing but not having much luck. Stoop to hoist a stone, wet and dripping, off the bottom. If a cer-tain food form is dominant, select a nymph that matches it as closely as you can. You might  even want to collect a specimen in a vial of alcohol, take it home, and tie a matching pattern of your own. It will rarely fail you, and it will give you a superb sense of satisfaction.

To capture insects that let go and drift away on the current when you lift a rock out of the water, you must use some sort of collecting net. You can buy one, or make one by stapling 3 feet of fine-mesh window screen to a couple of 4-foot dowels.

To collect with a net, spread the wings and plant the dowel ends on the bot-tom downstream from your posi-tion. Shuffle your feet in gravel, silt, or weeds up-stream from the net. Lift the net up and into the current toward you to trap what-ever insects it has collected. Carry it to shore. Look the meshes over closely. It helps to carry a small white-bot-tomed jar lid, a pair of tweezers, and a hand-held magnify-ing glass. Tweezer whatever you want to examine closely into the jar lid, and add water.

If you collect a wide variety of naturals, use a generic dressing that is close in size and shape and color to at least one or two of them. If you see a single dominant food form in your collecting, select an imitative fly that looks a lot like it.

Choose the right nymph for the situation, and you're likely to cradle a few more nice trout in your arms.

*T*hree basic rigs accomplish most nymphing. The first is unencumbered, with nothing but the nymph tied to the leader tip. This rig can be used with either a floating or sinking-tip line. The second is with the nymph at the tippet and a strike indicator fixed to the leader from 2 to 10 feet above the fly. This method is used with a floating line. The third and most common method for rigging nymphs is with a strike indicator and split shot on the leader above the fly. This method is also used only with a floating line.

Rigging with just the nymph is the simplest method, though it's often the most difficult to fish successfully because it's tough to tell when a trout takes the fly unless you fish with a tight line. Adding an indicator does not add any knots or much complication to the rig, but it increases dramatically the chance that you'll detect a take when you get one on a slack line. Adding both split shot and an indicator to the leader introduces a variety of options to rig differently for various fishing situations. The goal of this rig is to deliver your nymph directly to the bottom with the shot, and give it a free drift, while leaving the indicator bright and visible up top to let you know when you've had a take on the bottom.

All three rigging methods can be accomplished with the same simple set of knots.

The most common method for rigging nymphs is with split shot and a strike indicator on the leader above the nymph.

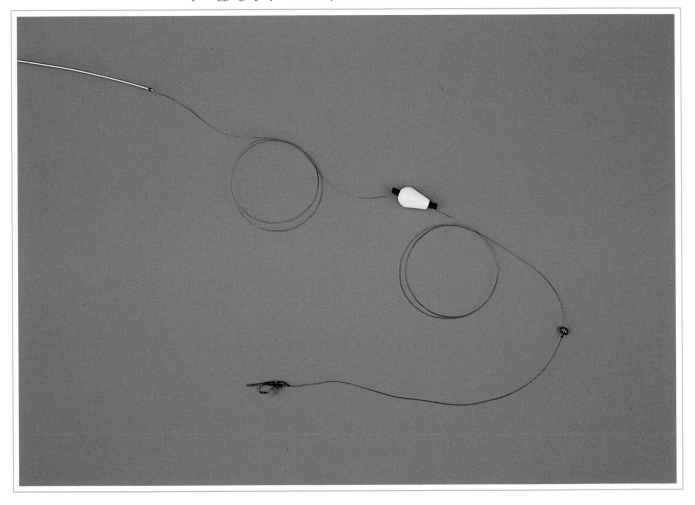

Knots for Nymph Fishing

You'll find just a few knots are necessary to fish nymphs for trout. Learn to tie them quickly and well, so that you reduce the time spent fumbling when you're out on the stream or lake, and also to reduce the number of fish that you lose because a knot came undone. The *reel knot* attaches backing to the reel spindle. The *nail knot* is used to tie the backing to the butt of the fly line, and to tie the leader butt to the line tip. The *barrel knot* and *surgeon's knot* are used to tie leader sections together, and to tie on tippets. The *Duncan loop* and *improved clinch knot* are used to tie nymphs to the tippet.

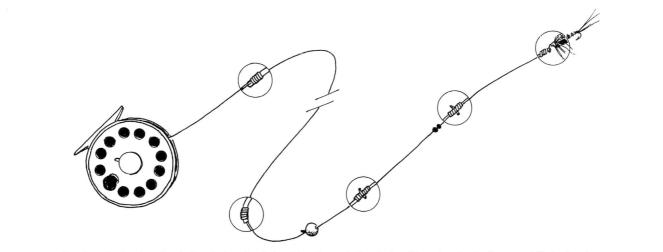

It takes just a few basic knots to attach backing to reel, line to backing, leader to line, and fly to leader.

Reel Knot

Run the backing line around the reel spindle and back out a few inches. Tie an overhand knot in the tip of the backing, and draw it down tight. This keeps the knot from slipping. Tie an overhand knot around the running end of the backing. This is no more than a slip knot. Draw it tight and snug it against the reel spindle.

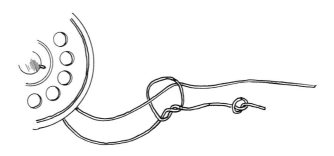

Nail Knot

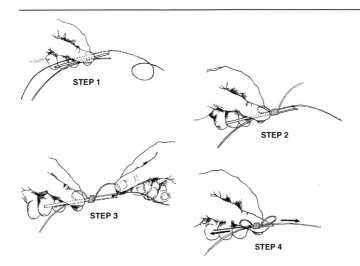

STEP 1

STEP 2

STEP 3

STEP 4

Lay a hollow tube alongside the line tip. Overlap a few inches of backing line or leader butt alongside the line tip and tube. Hold the overlap with your left hand and make 5 adjacent wraps of backing or leader around the tube and line, trapping them under your left forefinger and thumb as you go. Run the backing or leader tip through the tube and draw it snug. Pull the running end of the backing or leader to snug the 5 loops against the tube and line. Draw the tube out of the knot, and pull the tip and running ends of the backing or leader in opposite directions, seating the wraps tightly around the line. Clip the tag ends. (Test this and all other knots before fishing.)

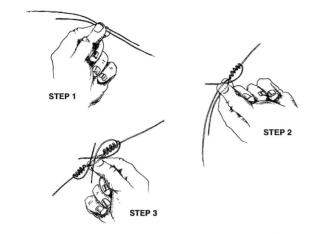

STEP 1

STEP 2

STEP 3

Barrel Knot

Overlap ends of leader a few inches. Pinch the overlap between your left thumb and forefinger. Use your right hand to wrap the tag end 5 times around the running end. Poke the tag end through the gap formed by the first wrap. Pinch the overlap between your right thumb and forefinger. Use your left hand to wrap the tag end 5 times around the running end. Poke the tag through the same gap in the opposite direction. Moisten the knot in your mouth, and draw the running ends away from each other to seat the knot firmly. Clip the tag ends.

Surgeon's Knot

Overlap the ends of the leader material a few inches. Make an overhand loop and draw the ends through. Draw the ends through the loop a second time. Moisten the knot in your mouth, and draw it tight. Clip the tag ends. (Note: The surgeon's knot works better than the barrel knot when you must join two leader sections that are more than .002" different in diameter.)

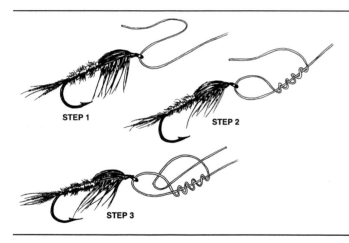

STEP 1

STEP 2

STEP 3

Improved Clinch Knot

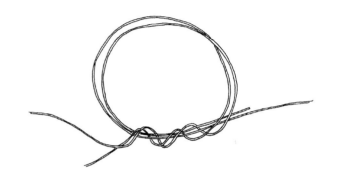

Run the tippet through the hook eye and draw it out a few inches. Make 5 wraps of the tag end around the running end. Poke the tip through the gap formed by the first wrap next to the hook eye. Poke the tip through the loop formed alongside the 5 wraps. Moisten the knot in your mouth, and draw it tight against the hook eye. Clip the tag end.

Duncan Loop

Run the leader tip through the hook eye, draw it out a few inches, and form a loop with the tag end next to the running end. Take 5 turns of the leader tip around the running end and through the inside of the loop you've just formed. Moisten the knot in your mouth, and draw the loops tight, leaving an open loop between the knot and the fly eye. (Note: The Duncan loop is excellent when you want to give the fly freedom to move. You can adjust the size of the loop by pulling the knot up or down the leader. When you catch a fish, the knot will pull tight to the hook eye. Pinch it between thumb and fingernail, and slide it to re-open the loop.)

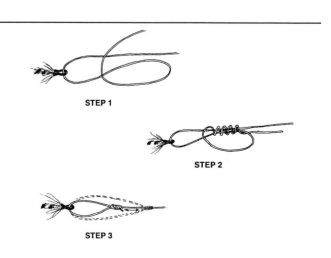

STEP 1

STEP 2

STEP 3

Rigging for the unencumbered nymph: Often, you'll want to fish an unweighted nymph inches deep, perhaps to trout feeding just subsurface, or a weighted nymph to trout feeding visibly along the bottom in shallow water. If you can see the trout, or their takes, you don't need an indicator. If you can get your nymph to the depth you want without adding weight to the leader, then it will fish better because it will drift more freely.

Rigging for indicator fishing: In many situations, you'll want to fish a nymph without weight on the leader, but with an indicator so you can tell when you've had a take. This will be especially true when you use weighted nymphs or bead-eyes, because they have enough inherent weight to sink deep.

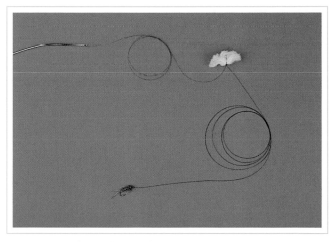

To rig an indicator but no shot, simply tie your fly to the leader, then fix a tuft of yarn or a hard indicator a few feet up the leader.

To rig the unencumbered nymph, simply tie it to the end of a leader the appropriate size to cast the fly.

When you don't need weight or an indicator, merely rig to fish a nymph as you would a dry fly. Use a floating line and tapered leader 8 to 10 feet long, with a two foot tippet. Refer to the chart on page 11 for the proper tippet diameter to balance the size nymph you're using. Tie the fly to the tippet with an improved clinch knot or Duncan loop.

When you fish a heavily-weighted nymph from a boat, casting it tight to the banks, you'll not want split shot or an indicator to get in your way. If you cast a sink-tip line, use a 4 to 6 foot leader. With a floating line, use a 6 to 8 foot leader. The tippet should be stout. Tie the fly to the leader with a Duncan loop. It is less likely than the improved clinch knot to weaken from constant flexing of the leader point because of the heavy nymph.

You will sometimes want to fish unweighted nymphs without weight on the leader, but with an indicator. This usually works best when trout are visible, or when they feed with visible rise forms, but you need help telling when they take your submerged nymph as opposed to a natural nymph near it. This often happens in situations where the trout feed in clear water; they'll be spooky. Use a tiny indicator, usually of yarn, for the light way it lands on the water.

To rig for nymphing with an indicator but no split shot, use a standard tapered leader, 8 to 10 feet long with a 2 to 3 foot tippet. Tie the fly to the tippet with an improved clinch knot or Duncan loop. Place your indicator on the leader 3 to 8 feet above the fly. If the indicator is yarn, merely make a slip knot loop in the leader, insert a small tuft of yarn, and draw the loop tight. Apply dry fly floatant and fluff the yarn.

It often works wonders to fish a nymph on the swing, down and across the current, with no shot or indicator attached.

In many situations, you don't need shot for depth, but you do need an indicator to detect takes.

Rigging for split shot and strike indicator nymphing: Shot and indicator nymphing is the core of modern nymph fishing. It's the nymphing method that will catch the most fish for you. It takes a bit of patience and practice to learn, but it's well worth the effort when you get it all together. If you're like me, you'll fumble with the method for some time, then things will suddenly and mysteriously fall into place for you. You won't know exactly what you're doing different, but you'll begin catching lots of trout on nymphs that you would never have known were down there in the past.

The shot and indicator technique has replaced the heavily-weighted nymph as the best way to fish the bottom in most situations. It allows an unweighted or lightly-weighted nymph to move freely at the end of its short tether to the shot. The fly drifts like a natural insect might. The method also assures that you'll truly be fishing the bottom, where trout hang out. With other methods, it's easy to think you're fishing the bottom when your nymph is actually lofted along a few feet above it.

The shot and indicator rig also replaces sinking lines as a way to get a nymph to the bottom in moving water, and still know when you've had a hit. The visible indicator moves when a trout takes your invisible fly. With sinking lines, you must feel a take in order to know about it. You can feel a take on a tight line, but a tight line prevents the nymph from drifting freely and fishing right. Sinking lines frequently present a Catch 22: if the fly is fishing correctly, you can't feel a take; if you keep a tight line to feel takes, you're not likely to get many.

To rig for strike indicator and split shot nymphing, start with a floating line, either double-taper or weight-forward. Normally you'll be using your all-around outfit, an 8-1/2 to 9 foot rod armed with a 5- or 6-weight line. If you're using a lighter or stouter outfit, the setup will be the same.

Use an 8 to 10 foot leader, the same one you'd use for dry fly fishing in the same water: tapered from a heavy butt section through a moderate mid-section down to a 2X (.009"), 3X (.008"), or 4X (.007") point section. This point would be your tippet in dry fly fishing, and should be a couple of feet long. Tie the nymph tippet to the point with the barrel knot or surgeon's knot. The tippet should be the right size for the fly, and one

When rigging for indicator and split shot fishing, be sure to use a nymph, split shot, and indicator that are in harmony, so the shot will get the fly to the bottom, and the indicator will support the weight of the fly and the shot without sinking.

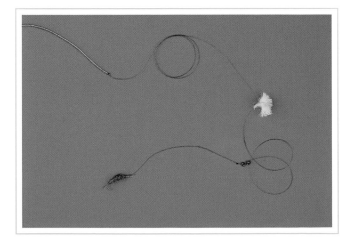

diameter smaller than the point, so adjust the size of your point according to the size tippet you want. Make the tippet just 8 to 10 inches long, no more than a foot. This keeps the nymph near the split shot, and therefore fishing near the bottom.

Slip a hard strike indicator up the leader and fix it in place with the end of a toothpick, or slip-knot a yarn indicator to the leader. Start with the indicator up the leader 2 to 3 times the depth of the water you'll be fishing. That's a rough rule; you'll move it higher in water that is faster or deeper, and lower in water that is slower or shallower. The heavier your nymph, or the more weight you use above it, the larger your indicator must be to support the weight and still float. Adjust the size of your indicator according to the amount of weight below it.

Tie your nymph to the tippet with the improved clinch knot, or use the Duncan loop if you'd like the fly to have more freedom of movement. Select two non-toxic split shot that total the right weight to get your fly to the bottom in the water where you begin fishing. By using two shot, you can remove one later if you move to fish shallower or slower water, and add one if you move to fish faster or deeper water. Pinch the shot just above the tippet knot. It will keep them from sliding down to join the nymph at the end of the tippet, which means you're no longer fishing, though it often takes a long time to notice it. Always watch the way your terminal gear strikes the water when you cast: you should see splashes for shot and for the fly. If you see just one, pull in and check to see if they're tangled.

Types of strike indicators: Your strike indicator has two tasks: to be visible to you, and to support your nymph and shot. You must be able to see the indicator move when a fish accepts the nymph. Yellow, orange, and chartreuse always work well. White, especially in a yarn indicator, is less frightening to trout because they see flecks of foam all the time. There is evidence that trout in heavily-fished waters are becoming shy of indicators. If that is true, use the smallest indicator you can. However,

Carry a variety of indicator types, for different situations. Include hard indicators, macrame yarn, and moldable putty.

an indicator usually does not disturb trout unless you land it on or near their heads, so always start with an indicator bright enough to be visible to you, and big enough to float with the amount of weight you're using.

Hard indicators such as Corkies, round cork balls of various sizes used in steelhead fishing, make excellent indicators.

They're holed in the center, and are fixed to the leader with toothpick ends, as are most commercial indicators made of cork or foam. Such indicators can be adjusted up or down the leader easily. Some hard indicators are split and held together with rubber bands. These can be removed without the need to run them all the way down the leader, forcing the removal of split shot and nymph. No matter which type of hard indicator you choose, carry them in three sizes: small, medium, and large.

A tuft of bright macrame yarn makes an excellent indicator. Tie it to the leader by forming a slip knot around it, then pulling the knot tight. Use scissors to trim it to the right size to float with the shot and nymph you're using. Dress the indicator with floatant, just as if it were a dry fly, and tease it into a fan. The biggest disadvantage of yarn indicators is their wind-resistance. A large one can require a 6- or 7-weight line to turn it over. Always trim your yarn indicator to the smallest size that will support the weight you're using. It's easier to cast, and also less disturbing to trout. A yarn indicator lands lightly on the water, and is the best type to use where trout are spooky.

Macrame yarn works well as a strike indicator. Slip knot it to the leader, and use scissors/pliers to trim it to the right size and shape, then . . .

. . . apply floatant to the yarn indicator, just as you would a dry fly.

If you use yarn indicators often, buy a combination pliers/scissors to replace your hemostat. You'll be able to de-barb hooks, release trout, and trim indicators with it.

Types of weight: Split shot is the most obvious type of weight to use for shot and indicator nymphing. Lead is fatal to waterfowl if ingested; use only non-toxic shot. Buy it in a dispenser that contains several sizes, letting you choose the right size to begin fishing with two shot. Be sure to buy removable shot, so you can take it off the leader easily. If you're nymphing right, you'll add and subtract shot often.

Weight comes in a variety of shapes and sizes. Use non-toxic shot, not lead. Twist-on weight and moldable putty also work well, and can substitute for split shot.

Twist-on weight comes in a matchbook type dispenser, and can be twisted around the leader just above the tippet knot. It's convenient to carry. You can adjust the amount of weight by pinching some off, or by adding a twist or two to what's already on the leader. It's lead, so it's not legal everywhere.

Various types of non-toxic soft weighting putty are designed to be molded to your leader around the tippet knot. Putty is easy to shape, less prone to snagging than most types of weight, and can be adjusted easily by adding or subtracting a pinch. If you use putty, keep a dab of it pasted to your rod handle. You can add or subtract weight in a hurry as you move from one depth or current speed to another.

Adjusting for depth of water and current speed: If you use too much weight, or place your indicator too high on the leader, your nymph will settle to the bottom and simply sit. If you use too little weight, or place your indicator too low on the leader, your nymph will drift far above the bottom. You must slowly learn to adjust the amount of weight and the position of the indicator for the speed and depth of the water you're fishing. Your goal is to rig so your nymph bounces along the bottom at the speed a natural insect would drift with the current.

It's a rough rule that the strike indicator should be placed up the leader 2 to 3 times the depth of the water fished, and that you should use just enough weight on the leader to get the fly to the bottom. That is an excellent starting point, but you'll need to fine tune it with the first few casts, adjusting for the speed of the current. Then you'll need to adjust constantly as you move from one piece of water to the next.

If you move to water that is deeper or faster, slip the indicator up toward the line tip 1 to 2 feet. If necessary, add a split shot or two, the same size as the ones you're already using. Sometimes it's necessary to add length to the leader in order

When you step into shallow water, and begin fishing the edges of any holding water, large or small, rig to fish for the depth in which your nymph will drift. That usually means placing the indicator a couple of times the depth of the water up the leader, but . . .

. . . when you move out to fish deeper water, you'll need to add more weight, and slip the indicator farther up the leader, in order to continue fishing your nymph on the bottom where trout will take it and put a bend in your rod.

to get the fly down in fast water that is deeper than 4 or 5 feet. Add 2 to 4 feet of leader to the point, and keep the tippet to the 8 to 12 inches it was before.

If you move to water that is shallower or slower, and begin hanging up on the bottom, slip the indicator one to three feet down the leader closer to the fly. Remove a shot or two from the leader. That is why you start with two small shot rather than a single large one: it makes it easier to adjust to the depth you're fishing.

Most folks fail to adjust their rigging for the water they're fishing, and also when they move from one water type to another. It's the critical key to nymphing success. As soon as you begin doing it, you automatically increase your success far beyond the average.

A simple rule to remember: if you're not catching fish, you're nearly always fishing too far above the bottom. Begin by moving the strike indicator up to a foot from your line tip. Then add a split shot. Fish for awhile. If you're still not catching fish, and not bumping bottom, add another shot. Keep adding weight until you begin bumping bottom or catching trout.

Two-nymph rigs: It's common and often smart to fish two nymphs on the same leader. This gives you the opportunity to offer the trout a choice between a large fly and a small one, a dark one and a light one, or some specific combination of imitations, say a scud and a midge nymph at the same time. You can also fish a bead-eye and a regular nymph to see which the

trout prefer. Some experienced nymph fishermen even add a third nymph, but be sure to see the following caution on casting before you try it.

You can use a two-nymph rig to fish the bottom without split shot. Use a large and heavily-weighted nymph for weight to deliver a small nymph to the bottom. You'll get most hits on the smaller fly, but you might pick up a few fish that aren't interested in such a small bite. These might be large trout, though it's far from true that you'll always catch big fish on big flies.

To rig with split shot and two nymphs, tie a tippet to the point, pinch split shot above the tippet knot, and tie the first nymph to the tippet. This is the normal rig for a single nymph.

Various types of two-nymph rigs help you explore the bottom while offering trout a choice between two sizes, two colors, or two styles.

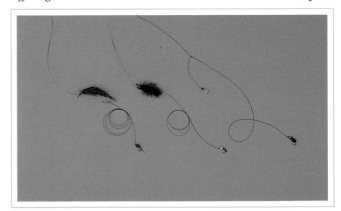

Now tie a second 8 to 12 inch tippet to the hook bend with an improved clinch knot. Tie the second nymph to this tippet with an improved clinch knot or Duncan loop.

To rig one large fly for weight and a small trailer, tie the large fly to the end of the point with the improved clinch knot or Duncan loop. Tie an 8 to 12 inch tippet to the bend of the large hook with an improved clinch knot. Tie the smaller fly to this tippet with an improved clinch knot or Duncan loop. If you'd like to add a third nymph, tie another tippet to the second hook bend, and tie the third fly to this tippet.

> **Caution on casting:** When you cast a 2- or 3-nymph rig, you have more things on your leader to tangle. Pay careful attention to the casting hints in Chapter 5, "Casting without Tangling". You must be able to cast with an open loop to avoid constant tangles.
>
> When you hand-land a trout with a 2- or 3-nymph rig, remember the extra hook or hooks dangling dangerously. Be careful to keep them away from your hand when you land the fish, and also when you release it, or you'll be the one hooked. Whenever possible, it's best for you and for the trout if you use a landing net.

Rigging for slack line nymphing: Author John Judy, in his book *Slack Line Strategies* (Stackpole Books, 1994), outlined a method for fishing a nymph with a leader hinged at a 90 degree angle at the indicator. The fly hangs straight down rather than trailing at a slight angle as it does when you rig normally for indicator and shot.

Use a large fan of yarn for the indicator in slack line nymphing. This floats like a flag and reacts to the slightest touch by a fish. The indicator is slip-knotted to the end of a heavy leader butt just 5 or 6 feet long. A tapered leader cut back works fine.

The tippet is a single length of leader a foot longer than the depth of the water, and the appropriate size for the fly you'll be

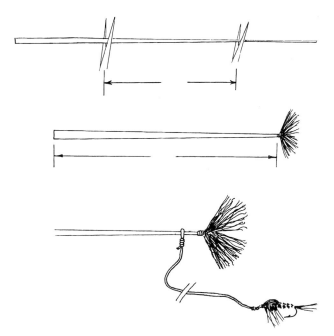

To rig for slack-line nymphing, use a large tuft of yarn clinch-knotted to the leader butt. Tie the tippet to this so that it hangs straight down, with a hinged effect.

fishing (see chart on page 11). Tie it to the leader butt with an improved clinch knot, and slide this knot against the indicator. The lighter the tippet the more quickly the fly will sink, and the more freedom it will have in its drift. It's not uncommon to fish the slack line method with 5 to 8 foot tippets in 4X and 5X, even for large trout.

Slack line nymphing works best with a medium to large weighted fly. You'll be able to get the fly down with far less weight than you'd usually need. If you find that you need some added weight on the leader, tie 8 to 12 inches of leader as a tippet, and use the tippet knot as the stop for whatever weight you need to add.

The slack line method is most effective on broad waters where depth is constant and the current flows at a relatively slow and even speed. In those types of waters, the method is deadly.

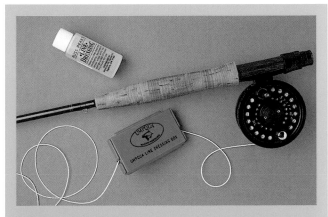

Keep your line clean: Few people clean and dress modern fly lines. It's a mistake. Lines still get dirty; when they do they sink, making line control much more difficult. Line control is critical to nymphing. Make it a habit to clean your line each day before you begin fishing.

Choose your rigging at waterside: Always wait until you reach the water you're going to fish before rigging up for nymphing. Look the water over carefully; judge its depth and the speed of its current. Then decide the best way to fish it. If you rig at the car, before scouting the water, chances are you'll rig wrong, but be too eager to get started fishing to stop and re-rig correctly. Then you're just pestering water that might be productive if you took time to rig for it and fish it right.

In nymphing, you face minor casting difficulties that are not present when you cast a dry fly, wet, or streamer. Most of the time, those flies are cast alone, and are not weighted. The addition of split shot and a strike indicator to your leader, or a heavily-weighted nymph flipping around at the end of it, add up to tangles if you do not learn some special casting techniques to prevent them.

Begin by realizing that a stiff and fast rod is a handicap, because it is designed to cast long with a tight line loop. To keep from tangling with weighted nymphs and split shot and indicators, your goal is to keep things separated with an open line loop. If you get tangles no matter how you cast, try overlining your rod to slow it down. If it's rated for a 4-weight, it likely will handle nymphs better with a weight-forward 5-weight, or even a double-taper 5-weight. Arm it with a 6-weight and you might discover you're suddenly holding the perfect peaceful nymphing rod in your hand. The same is true in 5-, 6-, and 7-weight rods: go at least one and sometimes two line weights higher, and you'll usually succeed in slowing them down to where they're suitable for nymphing.

With modern graphite rods, it's more common than not that the rod is better for nymph fishing when overlined. The author's prime rod for both dry flies and nymphs is an 8-1/2 foot graphite rated for a 4-weight, but fished with a double-taper floating 5-weight.

In dry fly fishing, you want to cast with a tight loop. Do that with anything extra on your leader, and you'll be constantly tangled.

In nymph fishing, your goal is to cast with an open loop, to keep split shot and indicator and weighted flies from tangling in the air.

THE BASIC FLY CAST: Before you can execute the casting changes necessary for nymphing, you must know how to make the basic fly cast. It's the casting stroke you already use, or will use, in all types of fly fishing. Slight variations make it work for nymphing. It's best to practice with a piece of yarn tied to your leader. Remember that most trout fall to casts at 25 to 45 feet, not 50 to 60.

The basic casting stroke: The basic cast consists of a back-cast and forecast. Each forecast and each backcast takes just three rod movements: loading the rod, powering the cast, and the rod drift. The proper fly cast is made up of a set of movements that are truly simple.

Begin your practice by stripping 25 feet of line from the reel. String it through the guides, lay it out on the lawn, and hold the line with your line hand near the first guide. Never allow slack between your line hand and the stripping guide. Grasp the rod handle comfortably in your rod hand, whether right or left, with your fingers wrapped around the handle and your thumb aligned along the top.

The proper rod grip. When fishing, the line should be locked over the trigger finger of the rod hand, as shown. When casting, hold the line so no slack forms between the line hand and the stripping guide.

The backcast: Point the rod down the line, with the tip low to the ground. Load the backcast by lifting the rod smoothly but

quickly to a 45° angle in front of you. Use your forearm; keep your wrist straight. This starts the line moving and places its weight against the rod tip.

Without pause, drive the rod firmly back into the power stroke. Use the strength of your forearm and shoulder, but keep your wrist straight. Stop powering the rod just after it has passed an angle straight overhead. If you stop at the right moment, the line will unfurl in a loop at rod height. If you drive your rod too far back and down, or break the stiffness of your wrist, the line will be driven into the ground rather than unfurling at rod-top height.

While the line loop unfurls in the air, let your rod drift back to a 45° angle behind you. The most common mistake in fly casting is continuing to power the rod in too wide an arc, rather than stopping the power, then letting the rod drift. If you power it downward behind you, the rod will drive the line and your fly to the ground behind you. If you do this while fishing, you'll smack your backcast onto the water, or into the bank.

The forecast: Begin your forecast just as the backcast straightens in the air behind you. Timing is very critical. Start too soon and you crack the whip, and your line; start too late and the line has time to sink toward the ground. Start when the last of the line loop is just about straight, and still at rod-tip height.

Load the rod for the forecast by bringing your casting fore-arm forward and moving the rod tip from 45° up to about 60°. This straightens and tightens the line in the air, placing its weight directly against the tip of the rod.

Power the forecast by driving the rod straight forward with the strength of your forearm, shoulder, and wrist. Do not drive the rod with just your wrist; it's not strong enough to do the job, and if you turn the wrist more than a tiny bit, you will once again drive the line toward the ground. Stop the power stroke when the rod is just in front of your shoulder, not much beyond straight overhead. The biggest mistake on the fore-cast, as on the backcast, is not stopping soon enough. The forecast line loop should unfurl at rod height, not down toward the ground, or the water when you're fishing.

Let the rod drift to a 45° angle in front of you in preparation for the next backcast. The forecast does one of two things:

The proper casting arc for the basic fly cast is relatively short, with the rod stopped at a high angle both in front and in back.

it either lets you extend your line, or it lets you deliver your fly to the water. If you need more line out, let a few feet slip between your fingers while the forecast loop unfurls in the air. If you already have enough line out for the cast you want to make, let the rod drop down parallel to the ground—the water when you're fishing—and the line will settle to it.

A second and subsequent back- and forecasts are used only when you want to extend the cast, and need more line in the air. Stop the rod on the forecast at 45°, and stop the line with your line hand after 3 to 8 feet have slipped through your fingers. Then load, power, and drift for the backcast, load, power, and drift for the forecast.

Aim the rod tip at the point where you want the fly to land. The line and fly will follow. Practice with short 25 and 30 foot casts. Don't try to extend the cast until you can make line loops unfurl front and back at rod tip height.

Loop control for nymph casting: To keep your split shot and strike indicator and one or two nymphs from tangling on your forecast and backcast, you need to cast with an open line loop. In dry fly fishing, you want a tight, quick loop.

To open the casting loop when fishing with shot and indicator, or with a heavily-weighted fly, open the casting arc in order to control the size of your line loop in the air.

To open the casting loop for nymphing, merely make your basic casting stroke longer and slower. This change in your basic cast drives the rod through a longer arc, which translates into a wider line loop in the air. Drive the rod through the longer arc with the same amount of force, but in a patient movement rather than an abrupt, quick movement.

You must be careful to power the rod nearly straight forward and straight back. Do not drop your rod tip on the forecast or backcast. That does not open the loop; it merely drives the line toward the ground, or the water, in front of you and behind you.

The patient backcast: Whenever you fish with weight on the leader, or with a heavily-weighted fly, you must wait until the backcast straightens out in the air before you begin the next forecast. If you begin the forecast too soon with indicator and shot, they will whip around the loop and snap back up into the line or leader. This causes terrible tangles.

If you begin the forecast too soon when using a big weighted nymph, it will whip down and draw your backcast down with it. On the forecast, the fly will scorch through at low level. If you fail to wait the backcast out, you'll pelt yourself in the head or wind up wearing the nymph in your earlobe. Be patient.

When you're casting with any kind of weight, make sure your line is heavy enough to slow the rod, and to carry the weight. Throw a high backcast, then wait an extra beat while the line loop straightens in the air behind you. Before long you'll feel when the time is right for the forecast. Until then, it helps if you turn and watch over your shoulder as the line loop unfurls in the air.

Cast short, with minimum forecasts and backcasts: Always wade into position as close as you can to the water you want to fish, rather than extending your cast to cover the water with longer casts. Distance decreases your control, and makes it harder to detect takes. Most of your nymphing casts for trout should be between 25 and 40 feet.

Keep your fore- and backcasts to a minimum. This reduces the chances you'll wind up in a tangle. Any cast that requires more than two backcasts is probably one on which you should wade closer.

To water load a cast, let the line straighten in the current below you, and point your rod down the line.

To make the water-loaded cast, simply bring your rod forward in a normal forecast, aiming it at the place where you want the fly to land.

Water loading the cast: In most nymph fishing, you cast upstream, fish the cast down past your position, and wind up with the rod and line pointing downstream. If you let the current tug the line straight, you can use the weight of the line in the water to load the rod for the next cast. Your power stroke on the forecast lifts the line off the water and propels it upstream. This is called water loading.

With water loading, you can usually make that one forecast the delivery stroke, placing the cast exactly where you want it. If one forecast will not do it, then you'll need at most one backcast in the air to extend the cast or re-direct it to where you want it to land. Water loading eliminates lots of tangles. It also causes you to fish out the lower half of each cast, thereby increasing the number of trout that you catch.

THE ROLL CAST: The roll cast works when you're backed against brush or trees, and cannot make a normal backcast. You can roll cast up to 35 or even 45 feet without letting the line go behind you.

Begin the roll cast by stripping the amount of line you want to cast off the reel, and drawing it beyond the rod tip. Let it lay on the water in front of you—this cast requires water tension; you cannot practice it on a lawn. Lift the rod and draw the tip back to an angle just behind your shoulder. The line will slide across the water, following the rod. When it has settled into a curve behind the rod, begin your roll cast.

The roll cast is the same rod movement as the basic forecast power stroke: a short, strong stroke that drives the rod through an arc from just behind your shoulder to just in front of it. Be sure to stop the power while the rod is still high enough to drive the line straight out, rather than down. The line will lift off the water and roll out in a hoop. The hoop should be in the air, not on the water.

The roll cast ends when the line straightens out and the fly, or the split shot, indicator, and fly, lands where you want it. If the first roll cast lands short, draw the rod behind your shoulder, let the line drop in a curve behind it, then drive another roll forward.

The roll cast is an excellent way to get a few feet of line out for the first time, after which you can use either normal fore- and backcasts, or water loaded casts, to nymph fish a stretch of water thoroughly.

Begin a roll cast by bringing your rod back behind your shoulder, which will draw the line into an arc under the rod.

When the arc has formed, make a normal forecast, stopping the rod high enough to make the loop roll out in the air rather than on the water.

At the end of the roll cast, your line should be straight on the water and the fly should be right where you want it.

Dealing with the inevitable tangle: You're going to get tangled at times, when fishing with split shot and strike indicator, no matter how good you get. I don't desire to tell you how many tangles I deal with in an average day nymph-ing. When you retrieve a bad bird's nest, first nip the fly off the end of your leader. This lets you back the end of the tippet through the tangle, and gets you free much faster. Tie the nymph back to the tippet, and you're fishing.

The first step in nymphing moving water is to locate trout, or potential lies for trout. If you fish all of the water blindly, you'll spend most of your time fishing where there are no trout. That reduces your chances of catching them.

SPOTTING TROUT: Often you'll be able to spot trout. It helps to wear polarized sunglasses. Sometimes trout will be seen hanging high in the water, feeding on nymphs just sub-surface. Other times you'll be able to spot them near the bottom in shallow water, either feeding or resting. Once in a while you'll notice tiny flashes, as if there were bits of tinfoil rolling along in the current. Those are the flanks of trout flashing as

they turn to take some bit of drifting food. They're the best indication of all that it's time to tie on a nymph.

READING WATER: Most times, you'll see no hint of trout at all. That's why it's necessary to learn to read water: to figure out where they're most likely to be. Many things mark the most promising places to find fish. A boulder in the current always has a soft spot in the flow above and below it; both are perfect lies for trout. The dropoff below a gravel shelf that cuts across the head of a riffle, run, or pool is always a most likely lie. Lots of food gets delivered there. A trench or shelf in the bottom, usually marked by a slick area on an otherwise riffled

Trout will rarely be this easy to spot, but if you watch carefully, you'll often see them, which will make it easier to fish for them.

Most times, you won't be able to spot trout. A general knowledge of holding lies will help you look at a stretch of water and decide quickly where trout are most likely to be found.

CHOOSING A METHOD: After you find visible fish, or read the water for likely lies, it's time to choose a nymphing method that suits the water you're about to fish. It's best to choose your method, and rig for it, after you've seen the water rather than before. You never know quite what conditions nature will toss at you, or what the trout might be doing, even on water you've fished often.

Subsurface nymphing: If you spot trout feeding at the top or near it, you will want to try for them with dry flies first, in which case you'll already have the right leader if you decide to switch to a nymph. Just nip off the dry fly, tie an unweighted or lightly-weighted nymph to the 2 foot tippet of your 8 to 12 foot dry fly leader, and you're ready to fish. Most of the time you'll fish upstream to visible trout. You can fish without an indicator, but you'll usually detect more takes if you slip knot a small tuft of bright yarn 3 to 6 feet up the leader from the fly.

surface, always gives trout shelter. It's a great place to bounce a nymph right on the bottom. Anything that obstructs the current marks a likely lie.

In many productive riffles and runs, usually two to four feet deep, the currents are an even sheet, and no obstructions to the current are visible. The rough surface, however, reflects a rocky bottom. Any choppy surface over water deep enough to hold trout is an indication there are lots of scattered lies down below. In this kind of water, you must set up a disciplined casting pattern that shows your nymph along as much of the bottom as possible, because you never know precisely where the trout might be holding.

You can often glance at water and tell that it's not going to hold any fish. Walk on past it, and you spend a lot more of your time fishing water that has potential to supply trout.

Empty water: About half of moving water never holds trout. If you save yourself the time spent fishing it, you automatically almost double your catch. Empty water is usually characterized by a deep slow current over an even and unfeatured bottom. The bottom is silty and the surface is therefore smooth. Much empty water is too shallow to give trout protection from overhead predation, or too fast to give trout shelter from a constant current. Trout rarely hold in such water unless a hatch attracts them there. Then you'll want to fish dries, not nymphs.

Shallow water nymphing: In water 1 to 3 feet deep, with a slow to moderate current, your best method is the weighted nymph on a floating line and an 8 to 9 foot leader. A bead-head nymph is often excellent in this kind of shallow water. Tie the fly to a 2 foot tippet. If you cast cross-stream and fish the fly down and around on the swing, you'll be able to feel takes. More often, you'll cast upstream and fish the fly dead drift to get it near the bottom. In that case, add a small indicator about twice the depth of the water up the leader.

In water 1 to 3 feet deep with a current that is brisk, the split shot and indicator method works best. Rig with an 8 to 10 foot leader, a 2 to 3 foot point, and an 8 to 12 inch tippet. Your nymph can be weighted or unweighted. Add just enough split shot or other weight to get the fly to the bottom. Choose an indicator, whether solid or yarn, that is just large enough to suspend the fly and the shot. Fish with upstream casts and downstream drifts.

The slack-line method works well in water 2 to 3 feet deep wherever the current has an even flow and is rumpled on top so your large indicator does not frighten fish. Cut your leader butt to 4 or 5 feet, tie a tuft of bright yarn at the end, and tie a level hinged tippet to the leader. The tippet for this method should be 6 to 12 inches longer than the water is deep. The nymph should be weighted, or you should add a minimum of split shot to the leader. This method is used with upstream casts and downstream drifts.

Deep water nymphing: In most moving water 3 to 6 feet deep, the split shot and indicator method will be most effective. Use a leader that is 9 to 12 feet long, with a 2 to 3 foot point and an 8 to 12 inch tippet. Choose a size shot that gets your fly to the bottom with two or three on the leader. That way you can remove one or add one as you move from water of one depth and speed to another. Start with your strike indicator twice the depth of the water up the leader. If the water is fast, slide it higher on the leader. It's common to fish fast and deep water with the strike indicator a foot or so from the line tip.

Deep water is an excellent place to try a two-nymph rig with an indicator. Use a big and heavy fly for weight, and a smaller nymph as a trailer.

The Brook's Method is effective in any water that is relatively deep and so fast that it's difficult to get a nymph down to the bottom.

The Brook's Method: The late Charles Brooks fished big Western waters for big trout. His method for fishing deep, fast water called for a long, powerful rod, a weight-forward 8- or 9-weight Hi-Density sink tip line, and a 4 to 5 foot leader stout enough to turn over a size 4 or 6 nymph weighted with 20 to 25 turns of lead wire. That's heavy!

Wade as deep as you dare in fast water. Let your line trail downstream, and water load the cast to lob the fly upstream just 15 to 25 feet. It will plunge to the bottom quickly. Raise the rod and gather line as the fly tumbles toward your position. Lower the rod and feed line into the drift after the fly passes your position. Keep the fly right on the bottom as long as possible. No indicator is needed; takes will be brutal; you'll feel them as thuds.

If no fish takes, let the current lift the fly off the bottom and water load the line, then place the next cast a foot or two out into the current from the cast before it.

Split shot and indicator nymphing: This method is the core of nymphing. It works in water that is shallow, medium, or deep. It is excellent in slow currents or those that rush right along. You must learn to adjust the amount of weight on your leader, and the length of leader between the indicator and the fly, as you fish different depths and current speeds. With these adjustments, however, you can fish the method in nearly any water type and catch trout. Here's how.

Position for the cast: It's important, before you make your first cast, that you wade into the right position to fish the water that you've read as holding trout. The ideal position is within 20 to 30 feet of the lie, downstream from it, and at an angle off to the side. Your cast should be short. Avoid casting straight upstream over trout that you've spotted, or over water that is shallow or at all clear. Your line flashing through the air, or your weight and fly landing on the water, will frighten the fish.

Position for cast.

The cast: Place the fly, split shot, and indicator upstream from the suspected position of the trout: upstream from the prime bit of bottom you'd like your nymph to bounce along. This gives the nymph time to sink to the bottom. If the water is shallow and slow, your best cast might be just 3 to 6 feet upstream from the lie. If the water is deeper, or somewhat faster, aim 6 to 12 feet upstream from the lie. If the water is deep and fast, you might have to cast as far as 15 to 20 feet upstream from the lie in order to get the fly to the bottom in time to fish the lie correctly.

Be sure to cast with a patient casting stroke, to give you an open line loop. If more than one backcast is necessary, let the line straighten behind you before bringing it forward for the delivery stroke.

The cast.

Follow and draw.

By drawing in line and lifting the rod, you draw slack out of the line and keep in contact with the indicator without affecting its drift. You are able to set the hook.

Mending and tending: To get a relatively free drift out of the indicator, it's almost always necessary to throw upstream and downstream mends with the line. To mend line, raise your rod to lift the line off the water, then flip or roll the rod in an arc in the direction you want to move the line. If the line is downstream from the indicator, mend it upstream. If the line is upstream from the indicator, toss a downstream mend to bring it back into line with the indicator.

Follow and draw: After the cast lands, your goal is to give the indicator approximately the same drift you might get out of a dry fly fished on the same water, and at the same time remain poised to set the hook if your indicator twitches. That free drift is your best signal that the nymph is getting the kind of natural drift that you'd like. If your indicator is tugged around by the line on the surface up above, then your nymph is being moved unnaturally along the bottom down below. That's the main reason you cast upstream, and fish the fly down toward your position: to sink the fly to the bottom, but also to give the indicator that free drift.

As the indicator drifts toward you, draw line in fast enough to keep all slack out. This is the same thing you do in dry fly fishing, for the same reason: if you don't keep excess slack out of the line, you'll never be able to set the hook when the indicator tells you a trout has intercepted the nymph. As the indicator floats toward you, lift the rod slowly and follow the indicator downstream.

Do whatever is necessary to keep your line as straight as possible toward the indicator, without excess slack and without hindering its movement. If your line draws tight and begins to impede the drift of the indicator, for example, tend the line by tossing slack onto the water between the rod tip and indicator.

Mending and tending.

Follow and feed: When the indicator drifts downstream to your position, you will have fished the part of the drift toward which you made your cast. However, trout might be hanging out in the water straight in front of you, sometimes nearly under your rod tip, and also in the water downstream from your position. Unless that water has no potential at all, you'll be wise to fish out the cast, since the fly is already on the bottom where you want it.

As the fly tumbled toward you, you slowly raised your rod and drew slack out of the line. To continue fishing the drift downstream, merely feed the slack back into the drift and slowly lower your rod.

Again, mend and tend the line to keep the indicator drifting freely. When all of the line has fed out, and the rod is lowered to the water, the line will draw tight and lift the nymph off the bottom. You are now in perfect position to water load for the next cast.

Water loading for the next cast: When you've finished the drift, with your rod lowered to the water and your line straight

Follow and feed.

below you, you're in perfect postion to begin the next cast. Never pass up the opportunity to make a water-loaded cast when you're rigged with more than a single fly on your leader. It prevents tangles, and saves time.

Take a moment to look upstream at where you want the next cast to land, usually a foot or two from the first. The line and fly follow the direction of the rod, so aim the rod where you want the fly to land, and make a slow forecast stroke that lifts the line out of the water and sends it in an open loop upstream.

The water load is a great way to keep casting to a minimum, and therefore fishing time, with the nymph down deep, to a maximum. However, many times the line dangling straight downstream cannot be lifted and directed at the angle you want it upstream, and you need to change the direction of the cast. In that case, make a water-loaded forecast, then use a normal back-and forecast sequence to change directions of the line in the air. It should take no more than one extra backcast to get the fly aimed where you want it.

Water loading.

Detecting takes: Success at shot and indicator nymphing is wrapped around knowing when a trout takes your nymph. Sometimes the indicator jerks right under and your arm jerks back in response. Most times the indications of a take are far more subtle: your indicator twitches upstream an inch, or dips under a second and resurfaces, or even keeps drifting downstream but hesitates briefly in relationship to the speed of the current around it.

The rule for setting the hook is simple: any time the indicator does anything the least bit strange, lift the rod to set the hook. You will set the hook several times for every trout that you hook, even after you're experienced. One day you'll suddenly begin setting the hook at indications so subtle you do not know yourself what caused you to do it. You'll hook trout, and not know why.

To set the hook while nymphing, raise the rod quickly but not brutally any time you see the slightest odd movement of the strike indicator.

If you set the hook constantly and it's bottom every time, then remove a split shot, or drop the indicator down the leader, or both. If nothing ever happens to cause you to set the hook, even erroneously, then add a shot or two, and raise the indicator up the leader, until you're hitting bottom now and then. It's common to fish an hour in water that seems to be barren of trout, only to adjust the depth at which you're fishing and suddenly find that the water is literally filled with willing fish.

Patterning the water: No matter what kind of water you're fishing, set up a disciplined casting pattern that shows your nymph, or pair of them, to all potential lies along the bottom. Place your first cast upstream at a slight angle from your position, and fish out the drift. Place your second cast so that the fly drifts down a lane just outside of the first drift. Each subsequent cast should cover the water just a foot or two farther out. Imagine the bottom to be a floor that you're painting with parallel brushstrokes: each cast strokes your nymph along a new bit of bottom, exactly next to the one you've just painted. Cover all the water you can with 25 to 35 foot casts, then wade to a new position and begin covering a new bit of bottom from there.

NYMPHING RIFFLES: Riffles are shallow and fast, usually one to four feet deep. Their cobbled bottoms are sometimes studded with larger rocks and even boulders. The surface reflects the roughness of the bottom: riffles are choppy on top. They are perfect for nymphing because they harbor myriads of aquatic insects that get knocked loose from their moorings and tumble along the bottom to become feed for trout.

Riffles can be divided roughly into two types: unfeatured and featured. Looking at them this way helps you decide on the best way to nymph a particular riffle.

Nymphing unfeatured riffles: If the bottom of a riffle consists of cobble or stones all of a similar size, and the flow is a constant speed and depth from one side to the other, then its surface will have the same chop throughout the length of the riffle. The surface of such a riffle will give you few hints about where trout might hold on its bottom.

Never overlook these unfeatured riffles. They are incredibly rich in insect life. Trout hold and feed anywhere they can find the least break from the current. They tend to be scattered. In order to find them, you must set up a disciplined casting pattern that shows your fly to all potential lies.

The shot and indicator method works best in unfeatured riffles. Rig with a size 12 to 16 weighted nymph, or a two-nymph rig with one large and one small fly. Use a large indicator that you can spot easily in the rough water. Adjust your weight and the placement of your indicator so that you bump bottom once or twice on every cast.

If the riffle can be waded easily, begin fishing at the downstream end. Reach what water you can with 25 to 35 foot casts from your first position. Fish out each cast both above and below you. Water load, and cast again to paint your fly in parallel strokes along the bottom. Wade upstream to a new position and fish it just as carefully.

If the current is so forceful that you cannot wade upstream, then begin near the top end of the riffle, but still make your casts upstream. Fish what water you can with short casts from the first position, then wade downstream a few feet before turning to fish back upstream to the new section of bottom.

When fishing an unfeatured riffle, cover all of the water with the shot and indicator method.

Nymphing featured riffles: Many riffles flow over a bottom of cobble and stone studded with boulders, ledges, trenches and other features that break the current, and mark obvious lies for trout. In such featured riffles, fish the water between lies just as you would an unfeatured riffle: adjusting your rigging right for the depth and current speed, then covering all of the bottom. But concentrate your casts when you reach those features that spell trout.

The best rigging is usually the same as for an unfeatured riffle: the split shot and indicator rig with one or two nymphs. The primary difference is in the care you'll take reading the water, and fishing those lies.

Sneak up close and drop your fly into the slack water behind every boulder. Float your indicator down the slick behind the boulder as if it were a dry fly. Cast to the current wedges on each side of the boulder. Cast a few feet above the pillow of water on the upstream side of the boulder, and let your nymph tumble downstream to the boulder along the bottom.

Look for current seams where two currents come together in a featured riffle. Use upstream casts to paint your nymph down the bottom on the near side of the seam, then down the center of it, and finally down the far side of the seam.

Slick spots in a riffle's choppy surface indicate ledges and trenches where the bottom has suddenly dropped away a foot or two. The current is broken; trout in pods of a half dozen or more hang out there because food is delivered conveniently in a place where they do not have to fight the force of the current. If you arrive at a ledge or trench marked by a slick on top, add a shot or slip your indicator a couple of feet up the leader, or you'll merely suspend your nymph over the heads of all those trout. You want your fly to reach the lip of the dropoff from upstream, then tumble right down into it, just as a natural insect might arrive.

Begin fishing at the downstream end of any featured riffle, if it's possible to wade it upstream. Wade as close as you can to all obvious lies. Fish them with short casts. Be aware of the need for constant adjustment of your weight and indicator as you move from one feature to the next.

NYMPHING RUNS: Runs in general are three to six feet deep, with minor gradients and therefore steady flows and relatively calm surfaces. They are slower and deeper than riffles; their surfaces are smoother and do not reflect quite so closely the structure of the bottom.

A run has less small cobble and more large rocks and boulders on the bottom. Some boulders break the surface, and mark obvious lies. More often, they are submerged but send slight boils up to the surface. These are also excellent lies, though less obvious.

In most runs, you can read the main flow, where the water is deepest and the current strongest, and get a broad idea where the run will hold most trout most of the time. It's often more difficult, however, to pin down specific lies in the average run with no obvious boulders. You do your best to eliminate empty water, for example edge water that is too shallow or has no current. Then you concentrate on carefully covering all of the bottom wherever you expect to find trout holding.

When fishing a featured riffle, concentrate your casts around lies such as boulders, or slicks that mark trenches in the bottom.

When fishing a run with no visible features, search for the main flow and fish so that your nymph covers all of the bottom under it.

Nymphing the main flow: The main current in a run is usually two to three feet deeper than the slower water off to the sides. That depth offers trout protection from overhead predation. The current tumbles food along the bottom, though runs are typically not so rich as riffles.

The main current of a run does not always flow down the center of the streambed or riverbed. In a bend, it will be pushed to the outside edge. In a straight stretch, it might meander from side to side. The main current will be constricted, and more obvious, at the head of a run where the current races in. It might dwindle and spread and be less obvious lower in the run. Your first task when reading a run with no obvious lies is to find this deepest and strongest current pulse.

When reading the main flow of a run, realize that trout will usually be most comfortable, and also best fed, along its edges. Most fish will be found under the current seam between fast water and slow. Trout will also crouch beneath the main flow itself wherever rocks and boulders break the current. They will rarely be found in the slow water more than a few feet off to the sides of the main flow. And they'll rarely be found anywhere except on the bottom. If the run is fastest at the upper end and slower the lower you go, then the trout are most likely to be found along the edges and toward the upper end of the run, because that is where the most food is delivered.

Rig to fish the main flow of a run with a setup that delivers your fly, or pair of them, quickly to the bottom and tumbles them along. The split shot and indicator method will normally be your best bet. Use a large indicator to suspend lots of weight. Use an 8 or 9 foot leader; don't hesitate to extend it to 10 or 12 feet on big, deep water. Use a 2 foot point, 8 to 12 inch tippet, and plenty of shot butted against the tippet knot. You won't make a mistake using two nymphs, usually one large and the other small.

It's very effective to use a heavy nymph for weight, rather than shot, in big and deep runs, especially if the river has a population of salmonfly nymphs. Tie the large nymph to the leader point, and a smaller nymph as the trailer.

Whichever method you choose, always be sure to use enough weight to get the fly to the bottom. Place your indicator far enough up the leader to keep the fly bouncing from place to place along the bottom.

Once you've got your rigging right to fish the bottom of the main current, then search it all, with heavy emphasis on the current seam between fast water and slow, right at the edge of the main flow. Take up your position at the lower end of the run, or at the lowest place you want to fish in the run. Often you'll want to insert yourself 50 to 100 feet below the head of a run, and fish the current seam from there to the top end. Pattern all of the bottom from your first position before wading upstream into a new position.

Make your casts upstream, and fish out the casts precisely as outlined for the strike and indicator method: follow and draw, mend and tend as the indicator drifts toward you, turn to follow and feed downstream, then water load for the next cast. When fishing the seam, place casts on the inside of it, then down the center, and finally on the outside—the current side—of it.

When you search for trout holding under the main current itself, be sure to get your nymph deep enough. It's often necessary to add a shot or even two in order to get down to those boulder lies that offer shelter to the trout. If you don't, then they'll never see your fly. When you've got the depth right to fish the main current, set up a disciplined casting pattern that covers all of the water. You don't know precisely where the trout will be holding under all that current.

In runs with very slow currents, you don't want to cast over the trout for fear of spooking them. You can use a version of the dry fly fisherman's reach cast. Cast downstream, and reach upstream with your rod while the line is still in the air.

After the nymph and indicator land, begin feeding line into the drift, and follow the drift downstream with the rod. This lets the nymph drift downstream along the bottom ahead of your line, and also lets you cast without throwing line over the heads of the holding trout. Try it over spooky trout; you'll begin fooling them a lot more often.

The slack-line method works best in runs, especially those with even depth and a constant current speed. Rig with a 4- to 5-foot leader butt, large yarn indicator, a hinged leader tippet a foot longer than the water is deep, and a fly with lots of weight. Make your cast nearly straight upstream, just as in shot and indicator nymphing. Subsequent casts should paint parallel brushstrokes along the bottom.

Follow each cast with an immediate upstream roll cast that is just strong enough to lift your indicator off the water and roll it upstream from the fly. This is the key difference between shot and indicator nymphing and slack line nymphing: the roll puts the indicator upstream from the fly, and allows the nymph to sink without hindrance. The fine hinged tippet also allows the fly to sink more quickly. The result: you are able to fish the bottom with less weight and a more natural drift.

If the water is shaped right for it, the slack line method is extremely effective.

In slack-line nymphing, make a normal upstream cast. The instant the line lands, throw an upstream roll.

This lifts the indicator and places it upstream from the nymph. This allows the nymph to sink freely, without hindrance from the indicator or line.

Nymphing specific lies: Wherever you see indications of a specific lie in a run, set up correctly for the depth and current speed of the lie, then fish it with a series of careful casts. The shot and indicator method will work well. A heavy nymph for weight to tug a smaller nymph down will be just as effective. The key is getting your fly, or flies, to the bottom quickly.

Float your indicator down the surface, therefore fishing your nymph along the bottom, on both sides and in the center of any current seam. Use repeated casts to make sure trout get a chance to see your fly. Drop your nymph and indicator in the slick downstream from any visible boulder, run it along both sides, and tumble it along the bottom to the upstream side of the boulder. If a boulder is not visible, but marked by a boil, the boulder will be upstream from the boil. Be sure to cast a few feet higher up into the current than you would to a visible boulder.

Wherever you see an obvious feature in a run, such as this boulder, fish it carefully.

If you see hints of a ledge or trench, marked by a slick on the surface, adjust to fish deeper, and get your nymph to the bottom of the dropoff. Cast upstream from the slick far enough so that your fly reaches the bottom in time to tumble into the suddenly deeper water that holds the trout.

It's critical, when fishing a run, to cast far enough upstream from any lie to get your fly to the bottom before it reaches the potential holding water. Don't cast right to a seam, boulder, or trench. Cast from 5 to 15 feet upstream, so the fly is on the bottom in the best water.

NYMPHING POOLS: Pools have three parts: the head, body, and tailout. Each must be nymphed differently. The head of a pool deepens from whatever water type, usually a riffle or run, that feeds into it. The body of a pool is deeper than the water upstream and downstream, though in a small stream that might be as shallow as three feet, in a large river as deep as twenty feet. In a tailout the water lifts up and gathers speed to flow into whatever type of water follows the pool, again usually a riffle or run.

Nymphing the head of a pool: The upper end of any pool usually has a current tongue feeding into it, carrying food to trout that wait along the bottom and off to each side.

You can nymph the head of a pool with an unencumbered nymph, either weighted or unweighted. Just tie the fly to your tippet. Cast almost straight out into the current, then let the nymph swing down and around. Mend or feed line to slow its drift if it gallops too fast. Fish it across the main current, then let it swim through the seam between the fast center current and the slower current at the edge. You can expect most hits just as the nymph crosses that seam.

You can also nymph the head of a pool by rigging for the split shot and indicator method, adjusting for the current speed and water depth that feed into the pool. Concentrate your upstream casts along the edge of the current tongue that feeds into the pool. If you're fishing small water, you can sometimes cast to the current seam on the far side of the current tongue, and fish out your downstream drift by lifting your rod high enough to loft the line off the faster water in the center current.

When fishing the head of a pool, rig for the type of water that feeds into the pool: a riffle, run, or current tongue.

When you fish the body of a pool, be sure to rig for fishing the bottom, because that's where the trout will hang out.

Nymphing the body of a pool: If the pool is not so deep that you can't get to the bottom by rigging with split shot and indicator, that method will work best for exploring its depths. Because the current in a pool is slow, you can usually get down to a depth about two-thirds the length of your leader. Since you can't extend your nymphing leader beyond about twelve feet when using indicator and weight, and retain control over your casting, the shot and indicator method is effective in pools down to about eight feet deep.

In pools deeper than that, it's best to rig with a sinking-tip or even a 30 foot sinking-head line. Use a 6 to 8 foot leader and a weighted nymph. Cast at a slight angle upstream from straight across. Give the line and fly plenty of time to sink to the bottom. Obviously this method works best in pools without much current.

The best retrieve is very slow. Your goal is to creep the fly along the bottom as slowly as a natural insect might crawl. Takes will be gentle pickups, and you'll have no indicator to tell you about them. Keep your rod low to the water, pointed right down the line, so that when a fish takes the fly you will feel it instantly. Set the hook before the fish has time to spit the artificial out.

Nymphing the tailout of a pool: Where the water lifts up and begins to gather speed at the foot of a pool, you revert to methods suited to the depth and current speed of that particular bit of water. This generally means the split shot and strike indicator method fished with upstream casts.

Swinging either a weighted or unweighted nymph across the current of the tailout can also work well. This simple method is especially effective at times when trout feed visibly, but refuse your attempts with dry flies. Try them with nymphs on the swing. You'll often be pleasantly surprised.

You can continue down to the tailout of a pool, and fish it with split shot and indicator. Often it works well to swing a nymph across the tailout with no shot or indicator attached.

Nymphing corners: Many riffles, runs, and pools have corner lies at their heads. A current seam forms between the faster main flow to the outside and the slower, shallower water on the inside. These corner pockets are perfect lies for trout. They can idle on the slow side of the seam and dash out to intercept food rushing by on the faster side. Often a pod of trout gathers along the quiet side of the seam.

Fish these corners carefully. Probe far up into water that looks too shallow to hold trout. The best method is indicator and shot fished upstream. You'll have to remove weight, and slip the indicator down the leader closer to the nymph, as you work your casts up closer to the shallow corner. Nymph the outside of the seam, and the seam itself, but concentrate on the slow current just inside the seam.

weighted nymph suspended beneath a large yarn indicator works well. The split shot and indicator setup will also take lots of trout. Use enough weight to get the fly down, and a large enough indicator to float without getting tugged under.

Wade as close as you can to a pocket, and fish it with short upstream casts. Tuck the nymph just behind boulders, or drop it just upstream from slicks that mark ledges and trenches. Hold your rod high to lift as much line off the water as you can. Constantly mend and tend your line to keep the indicator on the surface and floating freely. That is your sign that the fly is fishing correctly down below. Make repeated short casts; you never know when a pocket water trout will be looking the right way to see your fly.

Set the hook to any odd movement of the indicator, whether you think it's a trout or not. It's surprising how often what looks like the indicator's reaction to the nymph bumping the bottom turns out to be a nice pocket water trout that has seized your fly.

NYMPHING BANK WATER: Far more than half of all bank water fails to hold trout. They hold only along banks that combine three things: current to deliver food, depth to provide protection from predators, and obstructions such as boulders or indentations to provide shelter from the constant current. If you fish only where you find those three factors gathered, you'll automatically increase your take because you'll no longer waste time fishing water without any potential to provide trout.

Walking or wading the banks: Whether you rock-hop along the shore or wade out and cast back in, the best way to nymph bank water is to get close, cast short, and keep the drift of your nymph as near to the edge as you can.

NYMPHING POCKET WATER:

In whitewater cascades, and some swift riffles and runs, the water dashes so fast that trout have difficulty holding there. Boulders, shelves, and trenches—any obstructions to the current—form pockets in that fast water where trout can hold in comfort. The current trots food past the fish constantly; they dart out into the turbulence to take it, then retreat to their lies.

To read pocket water, look for boulders, or for slick spots on an otherwise bumpy surface denoting a ledge or trench below. Wherever you find an interruption in the current, you're likely to find a trout. Rig to get your fly to the bottom quickly. A heavily-

Always wade as close as you can to pocket water. Fish with short casts, heavy nymphs, and a high rod.

The most common mistake you'll make is to rig with too much weight, then fish too far out from the bank. Try a single weighted nymph in size 10 to 14. Use one of the basics: a Gold Ribbed Hare's Ear, Muskrat, Fox Squirrel, or Herl Nymph. Or try a bead-eye nymph; it will have just the right weight to penetrate the water quickly, but not so much that it sinks and snags on the bottom. Use a heavy nymph or lots of weight only if the water is deep and somewhat swift right at the bank.

Use the smallest indicator that will suspend your fly, to prevent disturbing trout. A small tuft of yarn is excellent. A large hairwing dry fly might be even better, since trout will often take it rather than the nymph. Fix the indicator three to five feet up the leader. If you use a dry fly, tie the nymph to a dropper tippet 18 to 20 inches long, clinch-knotted to the hook bend of the dry fly.

When you nymph bank water, cast close to the bank, and give your indicator a free drift along it, just as if it were a dry fly.

Make your first cast short and upstream, placing the nymph about five feet out from the edge. Work each subsequent cast nearer to the bank, until you're fishing six inches to a foot from it if the water is deep enough to allow it. Fish each cast downstream tight to the bank, giving your indicator that magical free drift. Retrieve line, and hold your rod high to lift line off the water.

Of course, if you see a boulder or other obstruction more than five feet out from the bank, pause to fish it carefully with a few casts above and below it before moving upstream to the next likely bit of bank water.

Boat fishing the banks: The first rule of nymphing banks from a boat is to have somebody else at the oars, positioning the boat perfectly about 30 to 40 feet out, at an angle that makes it easy for you to cast slightly behind the boat.

You'll usually use a big and heavily-weighted nymph for bashing the banks: something like a Bitch Creek or Girdle Bug. This is the prime place for your heavy rod, loaded with a floating weight-forward 7- or 8-weight line. Your leader should be eight to nine feet long, tapered to 2X or 3X. If you switch to a sinking-tip line, shorten the leader to four or five feet. Be sure to give your line time to straighten in the air on each backcast, or you'll beat the heavy fly against the boat, the guy rowing, or even yourself.

Watch ahead of the boat for water with current, depth, and an obstruction such as a boulder or indentation in the bank.

When you fish nymphs along the banks from a boat, be sure to cast at an angle behind the boat to get the best drift.

Where you find those three things gathered in one small spot, you'll have a prime lie. Hit it just as the boat passes it. Let the nymph sink a few seconds, then draw the line tight and retrieve just a few feet. Then lift the fly for the next cast, to the next bit of productive bank water.

Due to friction of water flowing against the bank, the fly lands in slightly slower water than that where the boat drifts. If you cast ahead of the boat, you'll catch up with the fly, introducing slack into the line. You'll never feel a take. By casting slightly behind the boat, you give the nymph a few seconds to sink; then the boat pulls the line tight and you can feel a hit if you get one, or retrieve a few feet if you don't.

Trout will often pounce the fly the instant it hits the water. You won't feel it because the line is not yet tight. Watch carefully: if your line tip jumps, set the hook with a wallop. That's a trout.

Nymphing to visible trout feeding on the bottom: At times, you'll spot trout feeding at or near the bottom. It's most common to spot them by the winks their flashing flanks send up as they turn to take naturals drifting on the current. If you see a lot of such winks, you've spotted a pod of feeding trout. If the water is shallow and clear, which it must be in order to see trout down there, then you need to make a careful approach and a delicate presentation.

Use an unweighted nymph if the water is shallow and slow enough to get it to the bottom, a weighted nymph if it's deeper or faster, or the split shot and indicator rig if the water is more than three feet deep or moving fast. Use the lightest and least obtrusive indicator possible.

Take your position downstream and off to the side of the trout. Cast at an angle upstream and across. If you cast straight upstream, your line flying over the fish and landing on the water above their heads will spook them. Place the cast far enough upstream from the trout so that the entry of the fly does not disturb them, and also to give the fly plenty of time to reach the bottom before reaching the position of the fish. The fly should tumble right down the drift lane of the trout.

Repeat the cast several times to give the trout plenty of chances to see the fly. If you still fail to interest them, try adjusting the amount of weight on the leader, or the placement of the indicator, before you change flies. Failure to interest trout is far more often a failure to reach bottom than it is a failure to find the right fly.

Most signs of an underwater take are subtle. Watch your line tip or strike indicator for any little movement. Watch for a wink on the bottom where you suspect your fly is drifting. Set the hook at anything suspicious. You'll be surprised how often some movement that you thought was not a take turns into a solid hookup when you raise the rod to query the trout: "Are you out there?"

If you see the winks of trout feeding along the bottom, stalk into position carefully, and show them generic nymphs bouncing right along the bottom, beneath a small indicator.

When you spot a cruising trout, cast far in front of it and let the nymph settle. When the trout moves near, animate the fly, make it look alive, and the trout will take it...when everything else has happened perfectly.

The induced take: If you spot a trout, or notice a lie that is highly likely to hold one, you can often con the trout by making your nymph move at just the right moment.

First, mark the precise location of the fish, or the suspected lie of the fish. Make your cast far enough upstream so that the fly arrives at the trout's position at its level. If it's on the bottom, the fly should come bumbling along the stones.

When the nymph reaches the depth of the trout and is right in front of its nose, stop your rod and lift it slightly to tighten the line. This starts the nymph swimming toward the top. It suddenly looks alive and about to escape; the trout takes it.

Nymphing to rising trout: You'll often find trout rising visibly, seeming to break the surface, but refusing dry flies. They're usually feeding on the nymphal or pupal form of whatever you see on the surface, but taking it just inches deep. When that happens, switch your dry for a mayfly nymph if mayflies are hatching, a caddis or midge pupa if adults of those are on the surface. The fly should be small, and unweighted or slightly weighted.

The best rigging is the dry fly leader with its long, fine tippet. Sometimes it helps to add a small strike indicator four to six feet from the nymph. An alternative nymphing rig is the dry fly with a nymph dropper. You're already rigged with a dry; it's easy to tie a 20-inch dropper tippet to the bend of the hook, then add the nymphal or pupal imitation of whatever your dry fly imitates. Your dry fly then becomes the marker for following the float of the nymph, and also the indicator when you get a take.

Present your nymph to rising trout exactly as you might a dry fly. Stalk the fish to within short casting range: 25 to 40 feet. Stay low and out of their sight. Approach them from downstream and off to the side at a slight angle, so your line will not fly over them in the air.

Make the cast three to six feet upstream from the fish, not more than a foot or so out of a direct line of drift down to the feeding fish. The nymph should drift unhindered, precisely as a dry fly might, right into the vision of the fish. If it looks at all like whatever the trout is taking, the fish will accept the fly. You'll see a visible riseform. Lift the rod to set the hook.

The cross-stream swing: If rising trout refuse a dead drift nymph, then move into a new position upstream and across from them, and deliver your fly on a cross-stream swing. This makes the fly appear to be alive and swimming. It's the wet fly method often derided as mere chuck-and-chance-it. That's foolish: the method presents a wet fly or shallow nymph just like an insect swimming feebly across the current, which lots of naturals happen to do.

Rig with a floating line, an eight to twelve foot leader and two to three foot tippet. Tie a weighted nymph to the tippet. You won't need an indicator, as you'll be able to feel strikes. Cast above and beyond the rising fish. If it's a single trout, cast about three feet past it and place the fly two feet above it. If you're working over a pod of fish, then cast so the fly swims just upstream from the uppermost of them. Lower the fly down the current a couple of feet with each subsequent cast.

Rising trout will often take a nymph fished shallow among their riseforms.

When the nymph lands on the water, simply let it begin swimming down and around on the current. If the current swims the fly too fast, make upstream mends to slow it. Swim the nymph slowly right through those rising trout. Sometimes takes will be solid thuds, other times they'll be soft. Either way, it's best to merely hold onto the rod and let the trout set the hook themselves.

If rising trout refuse dries, it often works to swing a nymph right through the rises.

NYMPHING SMALL STREAMS: Small stream nymphing offers a special reward. It's the schooling on nymphing that you get when you're forced to read the water so carefully, to figure out the right rig so conscientiously, and to place your fly so precisely to extract trout from tiny lies. That education can be transferred from the smallest and least-known stream to the most famous water, of any size, anywhere in the world.

Small-stream nymph rigs: If you use too much weight in most small-stream situations, you'll wind up with your nymph at rest on the bottom. To prevent this, use bead-eyes or moderately-weighted flies, and add shot only when you need extra weight. Your strike indicator should be small. Yarn lands on the water delicately, and is usually better than a hard indicator.

Begin with the indicator about three to four feet from the fly, and move it to five or six feet if needed. The closer it is, the more casting control you've got, so move it higher up the leader, for depth, only when you fail to get strikes in deep water.

A dry fly with a nymph dropper is a great way to fish small streams. Half the time you'll take trout on the dry fly, but don't complain. You'll catch more with the combination than you will with one or the other.

Small-stream tactics: Trout hold facing into the current, so your approach should be from downstream. Make a sneak into the closest position possible. This makes a precise presentation easier, and also gets more obstacles out of the way behind you.

Trout in small streams are almost always found holding on the bottom beneath the deepest current slot in a pool. This current will be in the center, or pushed against the bank to one side or the other. Begin at the lower end of it; make your first cast short, right up the center of it. Your indicator should drift down the current, over the deepest water, without hindrance, just as if it were a dry fly, which it might be.

Move upstream, and make subsequent casts higher into the main current. If the current seam is more than a couple of feet wide, make casts to cover each side of it before moving up.

When fishing a small stream pool, begin at the lower end, and fish your nymph in the deepest center slot.

Fishing plunge pools:
The average tiny stream, especially in mountain country, has a steep gradient, and plunges from pool to pool in slight waterfalls. The deepest water in any plunge pool is right below the falls. That's where the largest trout in the pool are likely to hang out.

To nymph plunge pools, use a weighted fly, or add a little extra weight to a leader about the length of your rod. Cast directly into the plunge. Let the falling water drive the nymph down with it. Lift your rod high to elevate the indicator to the surface, then follow it down as the nymph scours the bottom.

Trout can't see out of all that froth. Sometimes you can work up close enough to suspend the fly right under the rod tip. Hold the line off the water, watch the leader, lead the fly downstream. If the leader twitches, or if you feel a thump, raise the rod and you'll be engaged with a quick and lively small-stream trout.

Get up close and fish plunge pools with short casts, and hold the rod high to keep the indicator floating on top.

NYMPHING LARGE RIVERS: Fishing a large river can be intimidating until you realize that the biggest water, like the average trout stream, is merely made up of riffles, runs, and pools set between two banks. If you break a big river into its parts, and fish them one at a time, they're not intimidating at all.

Break a big river into its parts, fish each according to the rigging and methods that work best for it, and they are far less intimidating.

Nymphing large riffles: Shallow and fast stretches of the largest rivers are usually broad and uniformly choppy on top, with few features to mark where you might find trout. As in a riffle of any size, if you see a boulder or boil, a corner, or a slick on the surface that marks a trench down below, fish that particular bit of promising water very carefully.

In the unfeatured bulk of a big riffle, trout might hold anywhere, and they might be large trout. Set up a wading and casting pattern that lets you fish all of the bottom thoroughly. Show your nymph to all potential scattered lies. Be sure to rig with a leader that's long enough to let your flies reach the bottom, and use enough weight to get them there. Place your indicator high enough up the leader to dangle the flies as far as they need to go. If you fail to catch fish, add weight until you start bumping bottom on every cast.

Even the largest riffles, such as this brawling bit of water on the Deschutes River, can be fished easily by wading in the shallow water and nymphing along the edges.

Fishing big runs calls for cautious wading. Always be sure that your nymphs bounce the bottom in such difficult water.

Nymphing large runs: Runs in big rivers, especially if they have pushy currents, are among the most difficult waters to fish in any river. They are also among the most productive when fished with nymphs.

Cautious wading is mandatory in deep and strong water. Cinch a wading belt around your waist, and use a wading staff as a third leg. If you have trouble wading upstream, wade in at the head of a run, fish what water you can reach from there, then let the current ease you downstream a few feet before turning to cast upstream from the new position.

The best rig for a deep run is usually the split shot and indicator setup, with a pair of flies, one large and one small, suspended beneath an indicator large enough to keep them bouncing along. It's a good place to use your stout rod: a 7-weight or 8-weight will make it easier to cast large flies and lots of weight. Cast carefully to all holding lies, especially above and below exposed boulders and submerged boulders marked by boils.

A big run is also a good place to use the Brook's Method (see page 32). Rig with a sinking tip line, a short leader, and a large and heavily-weighted fly. Cast upstream and short, raise the rod and fish the fly down to you, then slowly lower the rod and feed line as the fly bumps the bottom past your position. Water load to lob the next cast back upstream, a foot or two out from the first.

The slack-line method (see page 38) is at its best in a large run with an even depth and current speed. Rig with a large yarn indicator, a heavy nymph, and a leader slightly longer than the water is deep. Cast upstream, and throw that initial roll to put the indicator upstream from the fly. Then fish the drift all the way downstream past your position, mending and tending the line as needed.

Nymphing large pools: In a large pool, the goal is to get a nymph down to the bottom and creep it along. Since you can only wade the edges, and the current will be slow, it's unlikely you'll be able to cast upstream and get a good downstream drift with an indicator. So the best way to fish a medium to large pool is to rig with a wet-tip or wet-head line, a short leader, and a heavily-weighted fly.

Cast as far as you can, aiming a little upstream from straight across. Give the nymph a quarter to a half minute or more of countdown time to sink. Then slowly retrieve the nymph toward you along the bottom. Be alert. Takes will sometimes be thumps. More often they'll be subtle. Most often the trout will be large.

The result of fishing a big pool in a big river can loom large when led toward your landing net.

SEARCHING FOR THE SWEET SPOT: In any reach of productive trout water, there's usually a single lie where the needs of trout for shelter from the current, protection from predators, and for an abundance of food are all met in one place. Such a sweet spot is called a prime lie. It will attract the largest trout from the surrounding water. When you find a sweet spot, and fish it just right, you're going to hook that trout.

The sweet spot in any bit of water might be marked by a boulder, a trench, or by two current seams merging, delivering food from two directions. Get into the habit of stalking the prime spot carefully and placing your first cast so that your fly fishes that precise place. You will deliver your fly first to the biggest fish around. When you fish the rest of the water first, smaller fish will whack your nymph, gallop around, and scare the one fish you'd truly like to catch. Fish for that big one first, if there's an obvious sweet spot, then go after those smaller ones later.

The sweet spot in any given piece of water will look slightly different, yet a lot like all other sweet spots. It will be defined by the deepest water in a lie, or by some feature that makes it a great place for trout to hold.

If you find the sweet spot in any stretch of water, the trout you catch there will be bigger than average for the water you're fishing, no matter where you fish.

Chapter 7

Fishing Nymphs in Lakes and Ponds

Lakes and ponds have no current to deliver food to trout. As a consequence, trout in stillwaters must travel to find food. Because food does not arrive on the current, specific holding lies offer no great advantages, and trout lose their territoriality. Rather than holding as relatively scattered singles, as they do most often in moving water, stillwater trout often travel in congenial pods of three or four to a dozen or more.

Stillwater trout migrate to various parts of a lake or pond in response to changes in the season, in the weather, and even to changes in the time of day. It helps you to find trout, and therefore to catch them, if you are aware of these major seasonal movements.

Cycle of the seasons: Trout respond to changes in water temperature and the availability of food by moving from the shallows to the depths, or from the depths into the shallows.

In winter trout reduce their metabolic activity and move into deep water, 15 to 30 feet down or even deeper if those depths are available to them. Due to the vagaries of water densities, the warmest water is found near the bottom in the cold of winter. Trout tend to sink and remain rather dormant unless a warm day and a rare hatch of insects, such as winter midges, tempts them to feed on top.

In spring and early summer, the sun warms the shallows and the lifeless bottom is suddenly not so attractive to trout. Spring turnover stirs a stew of nutrients into shallow water. A

The season of the year, current weather, and average air temperatures, will tell you a lot about where trout can be found in a lake.

myriad of aquatic food forms become active, begin traveling, feeding, and hatching in the shallows. Water two to ten feet deep becomes the best place to spend time if you're a trout. That's where you'll find them throughout the period when it's most pleasant and most productive to fish lakes and ponds: in spring and early summer.

In the heat of late summer and early fall, most lakes stratify. Water near the surface becomes too warm for trout. Again because of the peculiarities of water densities at different temperatures, the warm water stays on top while cooler water sinks to form a sudden dense layer 15 to 35 feet down. Water above this thermocline is too warm for trout; water below it has too little oxygen for them. So the thermocline becomes a barrier; trout drop down to it and suspend just above it.

In fall, water above the thermocline cools to the same temperature as water below it. When that happens, fall turnover stirs the lake's stew again, bringing cool water and fresh nutrients to the shallows. Trout, eager to feed after their time spent suspended in the barren middle depths, move back into the shallows and go on a feeding spree. This usually lasts until winter creeps up again, and the trout begin to drop down toward dormancy in the depths.

The result of all these seasonal movements is simple: in spring and early summer, trout can be found in the shallows; in the heat of summer and early fall, they suspend in the mid-depths; sometime in fall they move back into the shallows on a brief feeding spree; in winter they drop into the depths along the bottom and remain relatively dormant.

So you can see that during the most pleasant times of the year for fly fishing, trout are in the shallows, where it's also most pleasant to fish for them. When the weather is either uncomfortably hot or cold, a wise angler thinks about the depths. It's an excellent time to use a sinking line that delivers your fly down to a specific level and keeps it there, then to troll lazily in a float tube or pram.

The bottom of the shallows: When the season and the weather predict that trout will be in shallow water, but you don't see any fish cruising or feeding visibly, suspect that they're down on the bottom of the shallows. That's where sunlight strikes and vegetation takes root; insects eat the vegetation; trout find food most consistently there. In spring and early summer, then again in fall, when nothing happens to tempt them to the top, trout can be found resting, cruising, or feeding along the bottom, but still in water two to ten feet deep.

Concentrate on getting a nymph near the bottom of the shallows, and you'll begin catching a surprising number of trout during those periods that have been unproductive in your past.

Food forms and fly patterns: Some food forms that live in rivers and streams are similar to those that live in lakes and ponds. Many of your successful nymph patterns for moving water will work just as well in stillwater. Examples include those old basics, the Gold Ribbed Hare's Ear, Muskrat, Fox Squirrel, and Herl Nymph. They'll be most effective in lakes in sizes 10 through 14.

A few food forms that live in lakes are not common in streams, but often dominant in stillwaters. They are extremely important as food for trout, and therefore as models for successful stillwater fly patterns. These include scuds, damselfly nymphs, dragonfly nymphs, and midges.

Scuds: These crustaceans are found in nearly all stillwaters, at all times of year. They hang around thick weed beds, and

 sometimes scoot along the bottom. They turn to bright colors when dead, so you will see dressings for them in orange, pink, and white. But in their natural state, in the water where trout see  them and feed on them, they're typically olive or gray. Patterns for scuds should be tied in sizes 10 through 14.

Damselfly nymphs: Heavy populations of these predaceous nymphs creep about in submerged weed beds. When time

comes for their annual emergence, they migrate all the way to shore, where they find reed stems or protruding limbs on which they crawl out of the water. The adult escapes the nymphal shuck on plant stems or limbs, away from the water. Their migrations are often made en masse.

Trout will be glad to get a damsel nymph almost any time, but during a migration, usually in late May through June, they won't look at anything else. Damsel nymphs are usually green to olive-brown. They range in size from #8 to #12.

Dragonfly nymphs: These large stillwater nymphs are the aquatic stage of the large-eyed insects that will later clatter over the edges of your favorite lakes and ponds. The nymphs are an inch to two inches long, and

have a distinct hourglass shape. They hang out in vegetation

or along the bottom, hunting other insects. Because of their size, trout are always eager to get them. Imitate them with a Carey Special or Beaverpelt tied on a size 4 to 10 long-shank hook.

Midges: These insects are found in both stillwaters and streams. But they're more likely to prompt selective feeding in lakes and ponds, and you'll be saved from time to time if you carry a few dressings to match them. The most important stage is the pupa, that transitional moment between the larva that lives on the bottom and the adult midge that escapes through the surface.

Midge pupae rise slowly from the bottom toward the top; trout might take them anywhere between. But they concentrate just beneath the surface film, which is a difficult barrier for something so small.

They also get stuck in the surface film itself. You should have Midge Pupa patterns in black, red, green, and tan, some weighted to fish deep and others unweighted to fish near the surface. Tie them in sizes 14 through 18.

Tackle for lakes and ponds: If you're interested in buying a special outfit for lake and pond fishing, it should fall somewhere between your light and your heavy stream nymphing outfits. Because casting distance is often an advantage when fishing lakes, and never a disadvantage, satisfy that urge to own a rod that casts a weight-forward 6- or 7-weight line far off, with a tight loop. But don't feel disadvantaged if you must fish lakes with either the light or the heavy outfit that you already own. Choose the light if you don't fish in much wind; use the heavy if you live in country where the wind snorts. You'll be well armed.

More than 90 percent of your stream nymphing will be done with a floating line. You'll use a floating line a lot in lakes, too. However, you'll need a selection of lines that let you explore a wider range of depths in stillwater fishing. Add an intermediate line, which sinks very slowly, and a sinking-tip line, which will get your nymphs down a few feet and keep them there. If you intend to fish with full sinking lines, add a fast-sinking and an extra-fast sinker.

You might prefer to use a range of floating/sinking lines. Start with a floater, add a 10-foot wet-tip, 20-foot wet-belly, and 30-foot wet-head. The three sinking lines of this series should all be purchased in extra-fast sinking, to let you cover all water depths with them.

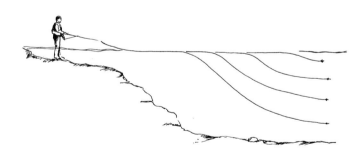

With a floating, 10-foot wet-tip, 20-foot wet-belly, and 30-foot wet-head lines, you can cover all the depths you'll need to in order to find trout in lakes.

Consider the advantages of a shooting head system: it takes up less room, requires fewer spare reel spools, and still lets you cover all the depths. You can buy a wallet that holds four shooting heads, and use a single reel with backing and 100 feet of running line already on the spool. The running line is fine, level fly line.

Each of the four heads is rated to sink at a different pace, from floating to intermediate to fast-sinking to extra-fast sinking. To change lines, and therefore the depth fished, just

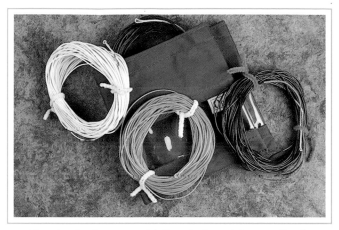

Shooting head system with lines in four sink rates: floating, intermediate, fast-sinking, and extra-fast sinking.

remove the current head from your backing, coil it and tuck it in the wallet, take out another. Uncoil it, loop it to the running line at one end and leader at the other, and you're ready to fish.

Leaders for nymphing stillwaters: If you use a floating or intermediate line, then extend your leader to between 10 and 12 feet, in order to give a weighted nymph opportunity to sink. If you use a sinking line, from a wet-tip to the deepest sinker in your shooting-head system, then shorten your leader to five to eight feet. There's no reason to plunge your line down deep if a long leader allows the fly to suspend itself far up above it.

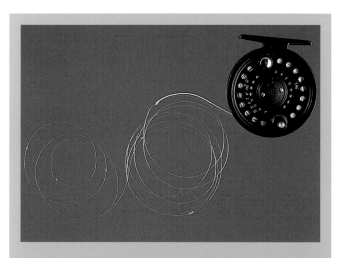

Always, always straighten your leader before you begin fishing with it in lakes and ponds. Stretch it between your hands, or run it over a patch of inner tube rubber: get rid of all those coils caused by memory of the leader's position on the reel. When you nymph moving water, the current or your split shot tug your leader straight. In stillwater, if you fail to stretch reel coils out of your leader, it will recoil in the water. When a trout takes your fly, all that slack must be taken out before you'll know you've had a hit. Most times the trout will spit out the fly before you ever know anything happened.

NYMPHING SHALLOW: During a large part of the trout fishing season, trout will be in shallow water and feeding close enough to the surface that you can nymph for them with a floating line, an intermediate, or a 10-foot wet-tip. You'll want to explore any structure such as rocky points, submerged logs, or the shoreline if no trout feed visibly. If you see trout either rising or cruising in shallow water, then you'll want to wade into position to intercept their movements.

It's usually smart to try visible trout with dry flies first, especially if they break the surface when they take something. But if dry flies fail, which they often will, try nymphs. You'll nearly always find the solution to taking a few trout.

Nymphing structure and the shoreline: Any sort of structure gives trout an obvious place to hide, and also gives you an obvious place to aim your casts. Look for floating logs, protruding logs, submerged logs. Look for boulders tumbled into the water from shore, or rocky points that step off into the depths. Cast to lily pad flats or reed forests that stand with their feet in water two to five feet deep.

The shoreline itself is the most obvious holding lie in lakes, unless the water is so shallow there that trout would find no protection from overhead predation. When nymphing tight to the shoreline, cast to dropoffs, any structure, and into the shade of overhanging trees. Fish such places carefully, but don't neglect the rest of the unfeatured shoreline. There might be invisible cover down there that you can't see. Even a small rock or fallen tree branch will give a trout a secure point from which to launch an ambush.

It's easiest to cover the shoreline if you have a float tube or pram, so you can cast toward shore rather than out away from it.

Rig for the shoreline and cover with a dry line if the water is two to three feet deep, with a wet-tip if the water deepens quickly near shore. It's best to fish from a float tube or pram, and to move slowly along the shoreline. Place casts as close to cover or the shore as you can. Let the nymph settle several seconds, watching your line tip carefully. If it twiches, set the hook. At least half of the trout you hook by casting to the shoreline will pounce the fly before you begin your retrieve, and therefore before you have a straight line and can feel the take.

If a trout does not take the fly as it sinks, retrieve it slowly. Coax it out a few feet, then give it a few feet of faster stripping retrieve. Most trout take within five to ten feet of cover or the shoreline. After that, it's best to lift your fly and place it about three feet down the shore from the cast before it.

If you have no float tube or boat, then probe structure and the shoreline from shore or by wading just a few feet out. Cover the water in a fan of casts from your position. But make the first casts of the fan right along shore, and retrieve parallel to it. It's a common mistake to walk right up to the bank and cast out as far as possible. That's a good way to scare the trout before you have a chance to catch them.

Don't make the common mistake, and hike right up to the shore, especially in the narrow cove of a lake. You'll frighten the fish you'd like to catch.

Nymphing to rises: Often you'll see stillwater trout rising, try to solve the situation with dry flies that match whatever is on the water, but discover that the trout won't accept anything you've got. Usually it's an indication they are feeding just sub-surface. It's time to offer them a nymph. Use the same rigging you've been using for the dry: a ten to twelve foot leader with a two to three foot tippet. Nip off the dry and tie on a small unweighted or slightly-weighted nymph the size and shape of the immature stage of whatever insect you see on the surface.

If trout feed sporadically, try placing your nymph right into a rise, as quickly as you can get it there. Let it sink a few seconds, then begin retrieving it with short strips: it should swim in three to five inch jumps. Be careful to watch your line tip and leader while the fly sinks, just after it lands. That's the most likely time for a take, and it's very difficult to notice.

If trout feed in a pod, it's better to cast to the near edge of the pod, let the fly sink, then retrieve it very slowly. In this way, trout see it not as it lands with a soft splat, but as they cruise casually into sight of it. Most often they'll nose over and take it.

If a single trout or pod feeds while cruising, try to calculate its direction and speed. Place the nymph several feet in front of it. Let the fly sink slowly, just a few inches. When you think the trout is near it, begin retrieving just fast enough to attract the trout's attention. Chances are it will race forward to whack the nymph.

When a trout strings two rises in a row, cast where you expect it to appear next, and begin your retrieve when you think the trout is in sight of your nymph.

Sight fishing to cruising trout: Two critical elements get involved when you stalk visible and cruising trout in the shallows of a lake or pond. The first is spotting the trout before they spot you. The second is then preventing the fish from seeing you as a danger, because they will inevitably see you.

To spot fish, wear sunglasses with polarized lenses. Wade into a position that gives you the best sight line into the water, depending on the angle of the sun. Wear a billed or wide-brimmed hat to keep out stray sun rays. Watch the water carefully; it takes awhile watching before you begin to see fish well.

To prevent trout spooking when they spot you, wear clothing that is not bright. The way you move is much more important than what you wear: keep your movements to a minimum; when you must move, do it slowly. Never send out wading waves, or float tube waves, that cross the cruising trout. If you do, they'll keep on cruising, but they'll also be aware of your presence, and far less likely to take. When you cast, tilt the rod over to the side to keep its movement out of the sight line of the trout.

Use a floating line and an unweighted or at most slightly-weighted nymph. The leader must be long—10 to 15 feet—and the tippet long and fine—3 to 4 feet of 5X to 6X. The fly should usually be small, size 14 to 18, though you'd be surprised how little difference pattern makes when you've got everything else worked out right.

Place your casts well ahead of a cruising trout. Don't let the trout see the line in the air or landing on the water. Let the fly sink while the fish approaches it. If the cast and its timing are perfect, the trout will see the fly sinking and turn to take it. If this does not happen, then give the fly the slowest of twitching retrieves. This will attract its attention. If the trout turns toward the fly, then gives the slightest turning motion, or you see the white of its mouth as it is opened and closed, set the hook gently. You'll usually come up against the solidity of a trout that is on, then up in the air or racing off toward the depths like a bonefish.

If the trout refuses your fly, then try another presentation. If you get more refusals, it's time to try another fly. Usually it's best to switch to one that is smaller and drabber. If you get constant refusals, run an aquarium net through the shallow vegetation, and see what comes up squirming in it. Match that, and you'll fool the fish.

Nymph placement: The ideal situation in sight fishing the shallows is a trout cruising toward you, or at an angle across your front. You can place the fly five to ten feet ahead of it without disturbing it. Wait till it's near the nymph, then animate the fly. The trout will usually nose over to take it.

The worst situation is a trout cruising directly away from you. It's tough to get the fly ahead of it without disturbing it. Instead, make the cast a foot behind the trout and two to three feet to one side. Plop the fly to the water with a slight smack. You'll either surprise the trout into turning around to take the fly, or you'll send it sailing. Either way, you've given yourself a chance to hook it.

When a visible trout is cruising straight away from you, try pipping your fly to the water just behind and off to the side of it, to attract its attention without spooking it.

![photograph of an angler standing in a lake with mountains behind]

When the light is right and the surface is smooth, you can often stalk the shallows slowly and carefully, and spot feeding trout. It might be the ultimate thrill in trout fishing on lakes.

FISHING NYMPHS DEEP: When trout are not feeding on the surface of a lake or pond, and are not cruising visibly just beneath the surface, you must do some exploring to find them. One of the most reliable tools you can use in that exploration is the nymph, or pair of them, on the end of your leader. Fish the shoreline first, and any visible structure. If that fails, then it's time to explore deeper. If you fish lakes much, you'll spend a lot of time doing that.

To find fish when they're deep enough to be out of sight, you must solve two problems: first locate the suspected level of the trout, and second get your fly down to that depth.

Locating trout when they're deep: The most likely place to find trout when they're down is on the bottom of the shallows. That is where they spend most of their idle time throughout the course of the trout fishing season. If the water is not warm enough to be stratified, and not cold enough to set the trout on the bottom and cryptic, they will usually be found in three to ten feet of water.

The first thing to explore for is vegetation. Recall the limits of light penetration: peer into the water to see where light no longer strikes through to the bottom, which means where you can no longer see it. Use polarized sunglasses. Cup your hands around your face to block any stray rays of sun. Look for any vegetation rooted to the bottom. If it's a dark day, drop your anchor over, pull it up, and see if any weeds are attached. Cast long, let your fly sink deep, and see where you begin picking up weeds.

On bright days, with the sun slanting into the water at the right angle, you'll be able to spot weed beds plainly. On other days, weed beds will show only as dark patches on the surface. These patches are often dismissed as the shadows of clouds. Don't make that mistake. Wherever you see a dark shade on the surface of a lake or pond, suspect a weed bed down below.

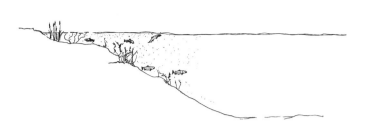

When trout are deep, they're nearly always associated with the bottom or with vegetation. Beyond the depths where vegetation takes root, you'll rarely find trout.

Fish your nymph over and around it. Weed beds are hotbeds for insects, and therefore trout.

While you're looking at the bottom, watch for any structure such as rock ledges, boulder gardens, or sunken logs: anything that might attract trout from the surrounding unfeatured bottom.

If the weather is hot, and you suspect the lake is stratified, you can sometimes discover the level at which trout will hold by patiently dropping a thermometer over the side, pulling it up quickly, and marking the depth at which the temperature drops a few degrees in just a few feet. That is the thermocline. Trout will not hold below it, because water there lacks oxygen. They suspend just above the thermocline because that's where the water is coolest. If the thermocline won't reveal itself to your probings with a thermometer, explore different depths with your fly, usually by selecting an extra-fast sinking line, then trolling patiently in a float tube or pram until you find fish. Constantly change the depth at which you explore. Start at around 15 feet down, and try depths to 25 feet.

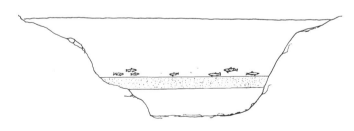

When a lake is stratified, trout suspend just above the thermocline.

The countdown method: The first step in getting your fly down to the correct depth is selecting a line with a sink rate that will deliver it deep enough. To fish just two to three feet deep, use a floating line, eight to ten foot leader, and weighted nymph. To get three to six feet down, use your wet-tip line, and shorten up the leader to six or eight feet. For depths of six to ten feet, use a 20-foot wet-belly line, a fast-sinking shooting

head, or a fast-sinking full sink line. To get down deeper than ten feet, use a 30-foot wet-head line, an extra-fast sinking shooting head, or an extra-fast full sinking fly line.

Once you've chosen the right line, then you've got to give it the right amount of time to sink. The first step is to make a long cast. On stillwaters, the farther you can cast, the more trout you can reach that have not been disturbed by your wading waves, or by waves from your tube or boat. Once the line lands, begin counting it down. Start with a count of fifteen seconds, and make your first slow retrieve. Add five seconds to each subsequent count until you catch a trout, pick up weeds, or get snagged on the bottom. Then shorten the count a few seconds and begin casting and retrieving in an arc around your position on shore, your float tube, or your boat. Cover all of the water in a semicircle around you, and you should find more trout at the same depth.

That's the beautiful thing about stillwaters: once you've found a fish or two, you'll usually find more in the same area, and at the same depth.

THE THREE VARIABLES IN STILLWATER FISHING: Lake and pond fishing seems a mystery. How do you find trout and catch them under all that vast expanse of uncharted and undifferentiated surface when they're not rising so that you can see them, and also see what they're eating? It's not so difficult as you might think. There are truly just three things that you must consider: fly pattern, depth fished, and speed of retrieve.

In stillwater nymph fishing, there are just three variables to solve: fly pattern, depth fished, and speed of retrieve.

Fly pattern selection: When trout are not feeding on something you can collect and observe, then you must choose a nymph based on your knowledge of common lake food forms, and the flies that look like them. That's why it's so wise to develop a small list of patterns that work well for you over the years: you can always tie on a fly in which you have great confidence.

When trout are down, you'll rarely go wrong choosing something like a Green Damsel Nymph in size 10 or 12. If that fails after half an hour or so, switch to an Olive or Gray Scud. A Midge Pupa in black, green, tan, or red is always an alternative. Consider adding a Midge Pupa as a trailer behind your larger fly, to double your chances of solving what fly pattern the trout want to wallop.

You'll develop your own small set of effective stillwater flies from the list of patterns in Chapter 8. When you do, then try your favorites for about half an hour each, until you find the one trout want.

Depth fished: After choosing a fly pattern, it's time to decide what depth to fish it. When the water is at the extremes of hot or cold, begin by fishing deep, with your fastest sinking line. Use the countdown method, and begin exploring at a fifteen second count, and add seconds on subsequent casts until you hit weeds or bottom or trout. If you hook one, you've found the right level.

If the water temperature is not at either extreme, below 45° or above 65°, then you look for trout on the bottom of the shallows, in water three to ten feet deep. Use a wet-tip or fast-sinking shooting head line to get the fly or flies down. The countdown method will help you find the right depth. Once you've found the bottom, you can begin exploring to locate trout.

Speed of retrieve: Now you've chosen a nymph pattern, or perhaps a pair of them, and a way to get down to the depth you want. It's time to figure out the speed at which you will retrieve.

The speed of retrieve should usually be based on the type of pattern you've picked. For example, a damselfly nymph should be fished with a short staccato twitching of the rod tip, followed by a pause, then a slow creeping retrieve. Repeat the sequence:

No matter what speed you retrieve your nymph, keep your rod low, pointed down the line, so that you can feel a take when you get one.

twitch the rod tip, pause, then inch line in to creep the fly along. With a scud pattern, retrieve with short strips while at the same time twitching the rod tip. This swims the fly in darts, like the natural. If that fails, try a patient hand-twist retrieve.

In general, try three speeds of retrieve. The first is a fairly fast stripping motion with the line hand, which swims the fly in six to twelve inch bursts. The second is shorter strips, somewhat slower, which swim the fly lazily along in four to six inch movements. The third is the hand twist retrieve, in which you roll your line hand over and over, gathering three to four inches of line with each roll. This movement should be very slow, so the fly creeps along at the pace of many natural aquatic insects.

You can layer a staccato twitching of the rod tip over each of these types of retrieve. This moves the nymph at the same pace, but in little jumps. Many natural insects swim this way.

It's always wise to experiment with each of the types of retrieve, until you find the right one. If none of the three basic speeds work, try adding the staccato twitching. Experiment, and the trout will tell you what they want.

Your single best investment for lake fishing: Most folks feel they need to rush out and buy a new fly rod for lake and pond fishing, plus a full set of sinking lines. Those things will help, but if you'd like to make a single investment that will be a lot cheaper, and catch a lot more trout for you, buy a float tube instead. You'll be able to reach water with your old rod and old lines that you could never reach with all the fanciest gear in the world without some way to get around on the water. Besides, float tubes are lots of fun.

Muskrat

Hook: 3X long, sizes 8-18
Thread: Black 6/0 or 8/0 nylon
Body: Muskrat fur
Legs: Speckled guinea fibers
Head: Black ostrich herl
Originator: Polly Rosborough

Herl Nymph

Hook: 3X long, sizes 10-16
Weight: 10-15 turns lead wire, optional
Thread: Black 6/0 or 8/0 nylon
Body: Peacock herl
Legs: Black hackle fibers
Thorax: Black ostrich herl

Fox Squirrel

Hook: 2X long, sizes 8-18
Weight: 8-12 turns fine lead wire, optional
Thread: Black 6/0 or 8/0 nylon
Tail: Red fox squirrel guard hairs
Rib: Fine oval gold tinsel
Abdomen: 1/2 red fox fur squirrel, 1/2 tan Antron
Hackle: Brown partridge
Thorax: Red fox squirrel fur with guard hairs
Originator: Dave Whitlock

Gold Ribbed Hare's Ear

Hook: 1X or 2X long, sizes 8-18
Weight: 8-12 turns lead wire, optional
Thread: Black 6/0 or 8/0 nylon
Tail: Hare's mask guard hairs
Rib: Fine oval gold tinsel
Body: Hare's ear dubbing
Wingcase: Mottled turkey quill (omit on sizes 14-18)
Thorax: Hare's ear dubbing

Olive Hare's Ear

Hook: 1X or 2X long, sizes 12-16
Weight: 8-12 turns fine lead wire, optional
Thread: Brown 6/0 or 8/0 nylon
Tail: Olive-dyed hare's mask guard hairs
Rib: Fine oval gold tinsel
Body: Olive hare's ear dubbing
Wingcase: Mottled turkey quill (omit on sizes 14-18)
Thorax: Brownish-olive hare's ear dubbing

Searching Nymphs

Hare's Ear Bead Eye

Hook: 1X or 2X long, sizes 8-16
Bead: Brass, to suit hook size
Weight: 8-12 turns fine lead wire, optional
Thread: Black 6/0 or 8/0 nylon
Tail: Hare's mask guard hairs
Rib: Fine oval gold tinsel
Body: Hare's ear dubbing
Wingcase: Mottled turkey quill (omit on sizes 14-16)
Thorax: Hare's ear dubbing

Peacock Bead Eye

Hook: 1X or 2X long, sizes 8-16
Bead: Brass, to suit hook size
Weight: 8-12 turns fine lead wire, optional
Thread: Black 6/0 or 8/0 nylon
Body: Peacock herl
Thorax: Brownish-olive fur

Olive Bead Eye

Hook: 1X or 2X long, sizes 8-16
Bead: Brass, to suit hook size
Weight: 8-12 turns fine lead wire, optional
Thread: Olive 6/0 or 8/0 nylon
Rib: Fine oval gold tinsel
Body: Olive fur
Thorax: Brownish-olive fur

Brassie

Hook: 1X or 2X long, sizes 10-18
Thread: Black 6/0 or 8/0 nylon
Body: Copper wire to suit hook size
Thorax: Muskrat fur with guard hairs
Originator: Gene Lynch

Zug Bug

Hook: 1X long, sizes 6-16
Weight: 8-12 turns lead wire, optional
Thread: Black 6/0 or 8/0 nylon
Tail: Peacock herl
Rib: Fine oval silver tinsel
Body: Peacock herl
Hackle: Furnace hen, sparse
Wingcase: Woodduck flank, clipped short
Originator: Cliff Zug

Near Enough

Hook: 3X long, sizes 8-16
Thread: Tan 3/0 Monocord or 6/0 nylon
Tail: Mallard flank fibers dyed tan
Body: Gray fox fur
Legs: Mallard flank fibers dyed tan
Wingcase: Butts of leg fibers, trimmed short
Originator: Polly Rosborough

Teeny Nymph

Hook: 1X long, sizes 4-14
Thread: Brown 3/0 Monocord or 6/0 nylon
Body: Pheasant center tail herl
Legs: Tips of body fibers
Originator: Jim Teeny

Prince Nymph

Hook: 1X or 2X long, sizes 8-14
Weight: 8-12 turns lead wire, optional
Thread: Black 6/0 or 8/0 nylon
Tail: Brown stripped goose, forked
Rib: Narrow Mylar tinsel, gold
Body: Peacock herl
Hackle: Brown hen, short
Wings: White stripped goose
Originator: Doug Prince

Bitch Creek Nymph

Hook: 3X long, sizes 2-10
Weight: 15-25 turns lead wire
Thread: Black 3/0 Monocord or 6/0 nylon
Tail: White rubber hackle
Body: Black and orange chenille, woven
Rib: Fine gold wire, over thorax
Thorax: Black chenille
Hackle: Brown, palmered over thorax
Antennae: White rubber hackle

Girdle Bug

Hook: 3X long, sizes 6-10
Weight: 15-25 turns lead wire
Thread: Black 6/0 or 8/0 nylon
Tail: Black rubber hackle
Body: Black chenille
Legs: Black rubber hackle

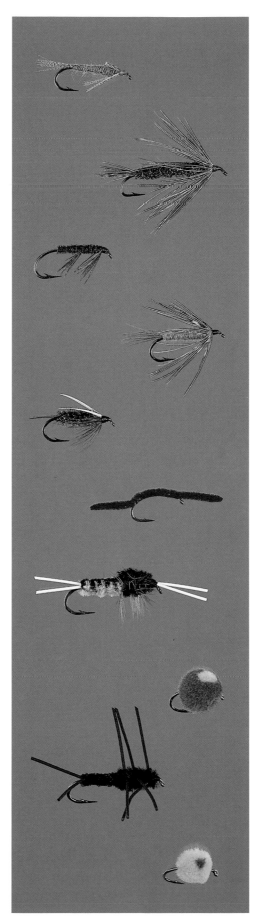

Carey Special

Hook: 3X long, sizes 4-12
Weight: 10-15 turns lead wire, optional
Thread: Olive 6/0 or 8/0 nylon
Tail: Ringneck pheasant back fibers
Rib: Fine gold wire
Body: Peacock herl
Hackle: Ringneck pheasant back feather
Originators: Lloyd Day and Tom Carey

Beaverpelt

Hook: 3X long, sizes 6-10
Weight: 10-15 turns lead wire, optional
Thread: Black 6/0 or 8/0 nylon
Tail: Ringneck pheasant rump fibers
Body: Dark beaver underfur
Hackle: Ringneck pheasant rump
Originator: Don E. Earnest

San Juan Worm, red

Hook: Curved shank, sizes 8-14
Thread: Fluorescent red 6/0 or 8/0 nylon
Body: Fluorescent red Vernille, ends burned

Glo Bug Orange

Hook: Short shank, sizes 8-14
Thread: Fluorescent orange single strand floss
Body: Flame glo bug yarn

Glo Bug Pink

Hook: Short shank, sizes 8-14
Thread: Fluorescent pink single strand floss
Body: Peach glo bug yarn
Eye: Orange glo bug yarn

Pheasant Tail

Hook: 1X long, sizes 10-18
Weight: 8-12 turns fine lead wire, optional
Thread: Brown 6/0 or 8/0 nylon
Tail: Ringneck pheasant tail fibers
Rib: Fine copper wire
Body: Ringneck pheasant tail fibers, as herl
Wingcase: Ringneck pheasant tail fibers
Thorax: Peacock herl
Legs: Tips of wingcase fibers
Originator: Al Troth

Flashback Pheasant Tail

Hook: 2X long, sizes 8-18
Weight: 8-12 turns fine lead wire, optional
Thread: Brown 6/0 or 8/0 nylon
Tail: Ringneck pheasant tail fibers
Shellback: Pearl Flashabou
Rib: Fine copper wire
Body: Ringneck pheasant tail fibers, as herl
Wingcase: Pearl Flashabou
Thorax: Peacock herl
Legs: Ringneck pheasant tail fibers

Hendrickson

Hook: 1X long, sizes 12-16
Weight: 8-12 turns lead wire, optional
Thread: Olive 6/0 or 8/0 nylon
Tail: Woodduck flank fibers
Rib: Fine gold wire
Body: Grayish-brown rabbit dubbing
Wingcase: Natural gray goose quill
Thorax: Grayish-brown rabbit dubbing
Legs: Brown partridge hackle

Quill Gordon

Hook: 1X long, sizes 10-14
Weight: 8-12 turns lead wire, optional
Thread: Olive 6/0 or 8/0 nylon
Tail: Two ringneck pheasant tail fibers
Rib: Brown thread
Body: Beaver belly fur
Wingcase: Mottled turkey wing quill
Thorax: Beaver belly fur
Legs: Brown partridge hackle fibers.

Timberline

Hook: 1X long, sizes 12-18
Weight: 8-12 turns lead wire, optional
Thread: Tan 6/0 or 8/0 nylon
Tail: Ringneck pheasant tail fibers
Rib: Fine copper wire
Body: 1/2 beaver, 1/2 gray goat or hare's ear, mixed
Wingcase: Ringneck pheasant tail fibers
Thorax: Same as body
Legs: Tips of wingcase fibers
Originator: Randall Kaufmann

Imitative Nymphs

March Brown

Hook: 1X long, sizes 12-16
Weight: 8-12 turns lead wire, optional
Thread: Orange 6/0 or 7/0 nylon
Tail: Ringneck pheasant tail fibers
Rib: Brown silk thread
Body: Amber goat fur
Wingcase: Ringneck pheasant tail fibers
Thorax: Amber goat fur
Legs: Brown partridge

Skip's Nymph Light

Hook: 2x long, sizes 8-20
Weight: 8-12 turns fine lead wire, optional
Thread: Brown 6/0 or 8/0 nylon
Tail: Ringneck pheasant tail fibers
Shellback: Ringneck pheasant tail fibers, dark side up
Rib: Fine copper wire
Body: Natural hare's ear fur
Wingcase: Ringneck pheasant tail fibers, dark side up
Thorax: Natural hare's ear fur
Originator: Skip Morris

Skip's Nymph Dark

Hook: 2X long, sizes 8-20
Weight: 8-12 turns fine lead wire, optional
Thread: Brown 6/0 or 8/0 nylon
Tail: Ringneck pheasant tail fibers
Shellback: Ringneck pheasant tail fibers, dark side up
Rib: Fine copper wire
Body: Dark brown hare's ear fur
Wingcase: Ringneck pheasant tail fibers, dark side up
Thorax: Dark brown hare's ear fur

Pale Morning Dun Floating Nymph

Hook: Standard dry fly, sizes 14-18
Thread: Tan 6/0 or 8/0 nylon
Tail: Ginger hackle fibers
Rib: Olive silk thread
Body: Yellowish-olive Antron
Wingcase: Gray Polypro dubbing
Legs: Ginger hackle fibers

Little Olive Floating Nymph

Hook: Standard dry fly, sizes 16-20
Thread: Olive 6/0 or 8/0 nylon
Tail: Blue dun hackle fibers
Body: Yellowish-olive Antron
Wingcase: Gray Polypro dubbing
Legs: Blue dun hackle fibers

Kaufmann's Black Stone

Hook: 3X or 4X long, size 2-12
Weight: 15-25 turns lead wire
Thread: Black 6/0 or 8/0 nylon
Tail: Two black stripped goose fibers
Rib: Black Swannundaze
Body: 1/2 black rabbit fur, 1/2 claret, brown, and black goat fur, mixed
Wingcase: Three sections of dark turkey
Thorax: Same as body
Antennae: Two black stripped goose fibers
Originator: Randall Kaufmann

Kaufmann's Golden Stone

Hook: 3X or 4X long, size 2-12
Weight: 15-25 turns lead wire
Thread: Gold 6/0 or 8/0 nylon
Tail: Two ginger stripped goose fibers
Rib: Pale ginger Swannundaze
Body: 1/2 golden brown rabbit fur, 1/2 amber, orange, and brown goat fur, mixed
Wingcase: Three sections of mottled turkey
Thorax: Same as body
Antennae: Two ginger stripped goose fibers
Originator: Randall Kaufmann

Box Canyon Stone

Hook: 3X long, size 2-10
Weight: 15-25 turns lead wire
Thread: Black 3/0 Monocord or 6/0 nylon
Tail: Dark brown stripped goose fibers
Body: Black yarn, twisted
Wingcase: Brown mottled turkey quill
Hackle: Furnace, over thorax
Thorax: Black yarn
Originator: Mims Barker

Brook's Stone

Hook: 3X or 4X long, sizes 4-12
Weight: 15-25 turns lead wire
Thread: Black 3/0 Monocord or 6/0 nylon
Tail: Black stripped goose fibers
Rib: Copper wire
Body: Black wool yarn
Hackle: One grizzly, one brown, in three spaced wraps over thorax
Gills: White ostrich herl, wrapped with hackle
Originator: Charles Brooks

Montana Stone

Hook: 3X long, sizes 6-10
Weight: 15-25 turns lead wire
Thread: Black 6/0 or 8/0 nylon
Tail: Black hackle fibers
Body: Black chenille
Wingcase: Black chenille
Hackle: Black, palmered over thorax
Thorax: Yellow chenille

Green Damsel

Hook: 3X or 4X long, sizes 10-12
Thread: Olive 3/0 Monocord or 6/0 nylon
Tail: Pale olive marabou
Body: Pale olive rabbit fur
Legs: Teal flank fibers dyed pale olive
Wingcase: Olive marabou one shade darker than tail
Originator: Polly Rosborough

Henry's Green Damsel

Hook: 3X long, sizes 10-12
Thread: Olive 3/0 Monocard
Eyes: 25# or 50# monofilament, heated to beads
Tail: Tips of olive Chickabou feather
Rib: Brass wire
Body: Remainder of Chickabou tail feather, wound as herl
Legs: Olive Chickabou tips
Thorax: Olive dubbing
Originator: Henry Hoffman

Green Caddis Larva

Hook: Curved shank, sizes 12-18
Weight: 8-15 turns lead wire
Thread: Black 6/0 or 8/0 nylon
Abdomen: Green fur or synthetic dubbing
Legs: Grouse hackle fibers
Thorax: Brown fur or synthetic dubbing

Tan Caddis Larva

Hook: Curved shank, sizes 12-18
Weight: 8-15 turns lead wire
Thread: Black 6/0 or 8/0 nylon
Abdomen: Tan fur or synthetic dubbing
Legs: Grouse hackle fibers
Thorax: Brown fur or synthetic dubbing

Peeking Caddis

Hook: 1X or 2X long, sizes 12-16
Weight: 8-15 turns lead wire
Thread: Black 6/0 or 8/0 nylon
Rib: Fine oval gold tinsel
Body: Natural hare's ear fur
Thorax: Olive rabbit fur
Legs: Ringneck pheasant back fibers
Head: Black ostrich herl
Originator: George Anderson

Deep Sparkle Pupa Green

Hook: Standard dry fly, sizes 12-18
Weight: 8-12 turns lead wire
Thread: Black 6/0 or 8/0 nylon
Underbody: 1/3 olive Antron, 2/3 bright green Antron, mixed
Overbody: Medium olive Antron yarn
Legs: Grouse hackle fibers
Head: Brown rabbit fur
Originator: Gary LaFontaine

Deep Sparkle Pupa Gray

Hook: Standard dry fly, sizes 12-18
Weight: 8-12 turns lead wire
Thread: Black 6/0 or 8/0 nylon
Underbody: Gray Antron dubbing
Overbody: Gray Antron yarn
Legs: Mallard flank fibers
Head: Gray rabbit fur
Originator: Gary LaFontaine

Ginger Emergent Sparkle Pupa

Hook: Standard dry fly, sizes 12-18
Thread: Black 6/0 or 8/0 nylon
Underbody: 1/2 gold Antron, 1/2 brown rabbit fur
Overbody: Gold Antron yarn
Trailing Shuck: Fibers of overbody yarn
Wing: Dark speckled deer hair
Head: Brown rabbit fur
Originator: Gary LaFontaine

Green Emergent Sparkle Pupa

Hook: Standard dry fly, sizes 12-18
Thread: Black 6/0 or 8/0 nylon
Underbody: 1/2 green Antron, 1/2 cream fur
Overbody: Green Antron yarn
Trailing shuck: Fibers of overbody yarn
Wing: Dark gray deer hair
Head: Brown rabbit fur
Originator: Gary LaFontaine

Cream Caddis Midge Nymph

Hook: 1X long, sizes 16-24
Thread: Brown 6/0 or 8/0 nylon
Body: Cream fur
Head: Peacock herl
Originator: Ed Koch

Olive Caddis Midge Nymph

Hook: 1X long, sizes 16-24
Thread: Black 6/0 or 8/0 nylon
Body: Olive fur
Head: Peacock herl
Originator: Ed Koch

Krystal Flash Green Rock Worm

Hook: 1X long, size 12-16
Thread: Brown 6/0 or 8/0 nylon
Body: Peacock green Krystal Flash, twisted and wrapped
Head: Brown rabbit dubbing
Originator: Rick Hafele

Waterboatman

Hook: 1X long, sizes 10-14
Weight: 4-8 turns lead wire, optional
Thread: Black
Tail: Brown partridge, short
Shellback: Metallic, bluish mallard secondary quill
Body: Red fox fur
Legs: Goose quill fibers

Backswimmer

Hook: 1X long, sizes 10-14
Thread: Olive 6/0 or 8/0 nylon
Shellback: Mottled turkey quill
Body: Olive tinsel chenille
Legs: Olive-dyed turkey quill fibers

Olive Scud

Hook: 1X long, sizes 8-16
Weight: 10-15 turns lead wire, optional
Thread: Olive 6/0 or 8/0 nylon
Tail: Olive hackle fibers
Shellback: Clear plastic
Rib: Olive thread
Body: Olive and gray fur, mixed
Antennae: Woodduck flank fibers

Gray Scud

Hook: 1X long, sizes 8-16
Weight: 10-15 turns lead wire, optional
Thread: Gray 6/0 or 8/0 nylon
Tail: Blue dun hackle fibers
Shellback: Clear plastic
Rib: Gray thread
Body: Gray fur
Antennae: Woodduck flank fibers

Pink Shrimp

Hook: Curved shank, sizes 12-18
Weight: 10-15 turns lead wire, optional
Tail: Fluorescent pink hackle, short
Rib: Clear monofilament
Shellback: Single strand Pearl Flashabou, with clear plastic pulled over
Body: Fluorescent pink Antron dubbing, picked out
Antennae: Fluorescent pink hackle fibers

Orange Shrimp

Hook: Curved shank, sizes 12-18
Weight: 10-15 turns lead wire, optional
Tail: Fluorescent orange hackle, short
Rib: Clear monofilament
Shellback: Single strand Pearl Flashabou, with clear plastic pulled over
Body: Fluorescent orange Antron dubbing, picked out
Antennae: Fluorescent orange hackle fibers

Black Midge Pupa

Hook: 1X long, sizes 12-20
Weight: 8-12 turns fine lead wire, optional
Thread: Black 6/0 or 8/0 nylon
Swimmer Paddles & Gills: White Polypro yarn, clipped short at back and front
Rib: Silver wire
Abdomen: Black fur dubbed tight
Thorax: Black fur dubbed roughly

Red Midge Pupa

Hook: 1X long, sizes 12-20
Weight: 8-12 turns fine lead wire, optional
Thread: Red 6/0 or 8/0 nylon
Swimmer Paddles & Gills: White Polypro yarn, clipped short at back and front
Rib: Silver wire
Abdomen: Red fur dubbed tight
Thorax: Red fur dubbed roughly

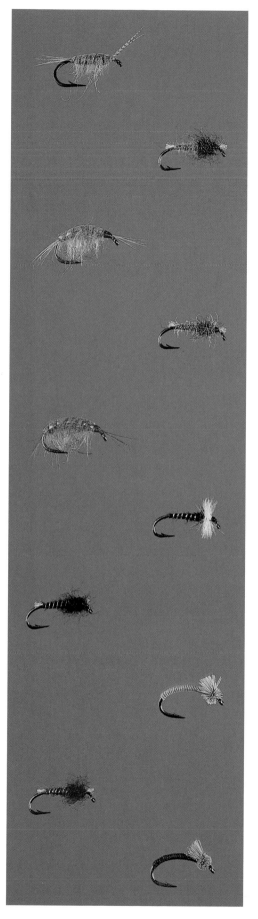

Green Midge Pupa

Hook: 1X long, sizes 12-20
Weight: 8-12 turns fine lead wire, optional
Thread: Brown 6/0 or 8/0 nylon
Swimmer Paddles & Gills: White Polypro yarn, clipped short at back and front
Rib: Gold wire
Abdomen: Olive fur dubbed tight
Thorax: Brown fur dubbed roughly

Tan Midge Pupa

Hook: 1X long, sizes 12-20
Weight: 8-12 turns fine lead wire, optional
Thread: Brown 6/0 or 8/0 nylon
Swimmer Paddles & Gills: White Polypro yarn, clipped short at back and front
Rib: Gold wire
Abdomen: Tan fur dubbed tight
Thorax: Brown fur dubbed roughly

TDC

Hook: 1X long, sizes 8-18
Thread: Black 6/0 or 8/0 nylon
Rib: Fine silver tinsel or wire
Abdomen: Black fur or twisted yarn
Thorax: Black fur, dubbed thick and loosely
Head: White ostrich herl
Originator: Richard B. Thompson

Tan Serendipity

Hook: Curved shank, sizes 14-22
Thread: Tan 6/0 or 8/0 nylon
Body: Tan Z-lon, twisted
Head: Natural gray deer hair, spun and clipped
Originator: Ross Marigold

Green Serendipity

Hook: Curved shank, sizes 14-22
Thread: Tan 6/0 or 8/0 nylon
Body: Bright green Z-lon, twisted
Head: Natural gray deer hair, spun and clipped
Originator: Ross Marigold

More Helpful Books for Fishing and Fly Tying

FEDERATION OF FLY FISHERS FLY PATTERN ENCYCLOPEDIA
Over 1600 of the Best Fly Patterns
Edited by Al & Gretchen Beatty

Simply stated, this book is a Federation of Fly Fishers' conclave taken to the next level, a level that allows the reader to enjoy the learning and sharing in the comfort of their own home. The flies, ideas, and techniques shared herein are from the "best of the best" demonstration fly tiers North America has to offer. The tiers are the famous as well as the unknown with one simple characteristic in common; they freely share their knowledge. Many of the unpublished patterns in this book contain materials, tips, tricks, or gems of information never before seen.

As you leaf through these pages, you will get from them just what you would if you spent time in the fly tying area at any FFF function. At such a show, if you dedicate time to observing the individual tiers, you can learn the information, tips, or tricks they are demonstrating. All of this knowledge can be found in *Federation of Fly Fishers Fly Pattern Encyclopedia* so get comfortable and get ready to improve upon your fly tying technique with the help of some of North America's best fly tiers. Full color, 8 1/2 x 11 inches, 232 pages.
SB: $39.95 ISBN: 1-57188-208-1

NEW YORK FLY FISHING GUIDE
Robert W. Streeter

Mention New York and most people think: concrete, sirens, and yellow cabs. This is true of a small area, however the Empire State also includes big woods, wonderful rivers, crystal-clear lakes, and great fishing. In this book Rob shares: the state's moving and still waters; species you'll encounter; access; fly plates, histories of the famed waters of American fly-fishing pioneers Theodore Gordon and Lee Wulff; general regulations; effective presentations; extensive list of resources; and more. New York State fishing has a fascinating history, spectacular surroundings, and varied fisheries, if you are fortunate enough to live or visit there, let this book be your guide. 8 1/2 x 11 inches, 113 pages.
SB: $19.95   ISBN: 1-57188-157-3

STRIPER MOON
J. Kenney Abrames

This is a beautifully written, all-color book about coast wade fly fishing (near the shore) for striped bass. Abrames explains tides and baitfish and covers techniques, reading the water, and the flies to use (shown in color and with pattern dressings). The author has a deep love and understanding of the fishery and I guarantee that you will want to fly fish for these wonderful fish after you read it! 8 1/2 x 11 inches, 48 pages
SB: $15.95   ISBN: 1-878175-67-X

SALTWATER GAME FISHES OF THE WORLD
Bob Dunn and Peter Goadby

This is a book for all those who love the sea and the great oceanic and inshore fishes which inhabit it. It is a book, not only for anglers, but for marine scientists, nature lovers and seafarers of all nations who share a curiosity about these majestic creatures and how our knowledge of them slowly developed over the past two millennia. A 2000 year history of the early naturalist and fishes they first described. Illustrations are intensely evocative of the period and remind us of the skills of yesteryear, now largely lost. There is the never-told-before history of the ancient sport of sea fishing from its origins in the mists of antiquity to the present day. All color, 9.5 x 12.5 inches, 304 pages.
HB: $89.95   ISBN: 1-86513-010-9

VIRGINIA BLUE-RIBBON FLY FISHING GUIDE
Harry Murray

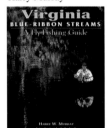

Virginia has a rich and vibrant history—President Hoover used to catch trout in the Blue Ridge Mountains to "wash his soul"—and a fishery to match it. The cool, clear waters of Virginia have much to offer the angler. Stream by stream, Harry Murray details their geography; the fish they hold; where and how to fish them; extensive resources; productive flies and presentations; and more. Virginia *is* for lovers—lovers of great angling in beautiful surroundings. 8 1/2 x 11 inches, 96 pages.
SB: $24.95   ISBN: 1-57188-159-X

HATCH GUIDE FOR NEW ENGLAND STREAMS
Thomas Ames, Jr.

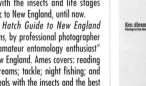

New England's streams, and the insects and fish that inhabit them, have their own unique qualities. Their flowing waters support an amazing diversity of insect species from all of the major orders—in fact, at last count, Maine, alone, has 162 species of mayflies, the most of any state. Few, if any, books deal with the insects and life stages specific to New England, until now.

Hatch Guide to New England Streams, by professional photographer and "amateur entomology enthusiast" Thomas Ames, explores the insects of New England. Ames covers: reading water; presentations for New England streams; tackle; night fishing; and more. The bulk of this book, however, deals with the insects and the best flies to imitate them. Similar in style to Jim Schollmeyer's successful "Hatch Guide" series, Ames discusses the natural and its behaviors on the left-hand page and the three best flies to imitate it on the right, including proper size and effective techniques. Tom's color photography of the naturals and their imitations is superb, making this book as beautiful as it is useful. A must for all New England fly-fishers! Full color. 4 1/8 x 6 1/8 inches, 272 pages; insect and fly plates.
SB: $19.95   ISBN: 1-57188-210-3
HB: $29.95   ISBN: 1-57188-220-0

THE FLY TIER'S BENCHSIDE REFERENCE TO TECHNIQUES AND DRESSING STYLES
Ted Leeson and Jim Schollmeyer

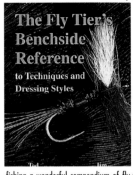

Printed in full color on top-quality paper, this book features over 3,000 color photographs and over 400,000 words describing and showing, step-by-step, hundreds of fly-tying techniques! Leeson and Schollmeyer have collaborated to produce this masterful volume which will be the standard fly-tying reference book for the entire trout-fishing world. Through enormous effort on their part they bring to all who love flies and fly fishing a wonderful compendium of fly-tying knowledge. Every fly tier should have this book in their library! All color, 8 1/2 by 11 inches, 464 pages, over 3,000 color photographs, index, hardbound with dust jacket.
HB: $100.00.   ISBN: 1-57188-126-3

STRIPERS AND STREAMERS
Ray Bondorew
Introduction by Lefty Kreh

The striper is the ideal fish for the saltwater fly-rodder. In *Stripers and Streamers*, Bondorew shares his nearly forty years experience, giving us an in-depth look at what it takes to be a successful striped bass fly fisher, including: a history of both the sport and the fish, identifying the various water environs of stripers, proper presentations and flies, how paying special attention to the moon, wind, tides, current, and even the behaviors of birds and surfers, can provide clues to make you a well-informed striper fly fisher. *Stripers and Streamers* is the most up-to-date treatment of this fast-growing sport, with plenty for both beginner and expert alike! All-color, 5 1/2 x 8 1/2 inches, 120 pages.
SB: $19.95   ISBN: 1-57188-072-0

A PERFECT FISH
Ken Abrames

Take your fly tying a step further; not only will you catch more stripers and other game fish, but tying flies will take on a more personal and satisfying dimension for you, and as we all know confidence is the name of the game. Abrames shares: the freedom and creativity in fly design; techniques for successful fly fishing; many productive patterns and how to tie them; much information on game fish behavior; deep insight into stripers and the flies that catch them; and more.

Abrames introduces you to a whole new level in fly tying—harnessing your creativity and intelligence to make for more effective flies. 8 1/2 x 11 inches; 110 pages.
SB: $29.95   ISBN: 1-57188-138-7
HB: $39.95   ISBN: 1-57188-179-4

Ask for these books at your local fly/tackle shop or call toll-free to order:
1-800-541-9498 (8-5 p.s.t.) • www.amatobooks.com
Frank Amato Publications, Inc. • P.O. Box 82112 • Portland, Oregon 97282

0061